T0046028

RELYING ON THE HOLY SPIRIT

DISCOVER WHO HE IS AND HOW HE WORKS

CHARLES F. STANLEY

HarperChristian
Resources

Relying on the Holy Spirit
Charles F. Stanley Bible Study Series
© 1996, 2008, 2019 by Charles F. Stanley

Requests for information should be addressed to:
HarperChristian Resources, 3900 Sparks Dr. SE, Grand Rapids, Michigan 49546

ISBN 978-0-310-10661-6 (softcover)
ISBN 978-0-310-10662-3 (ebook)

All Scripture quotations are taken from the New King James Version. ® Copyright © 1982 by Thomas Nelson. Used by permission. All rights reserved worldwide.

Any internet addresses (websites, blogs, etc.) and telephone numbers in this study guide are offered as a resource. They are not intended in any way to be or imply an endorsement by HarperChristian Resources, nor does HarperChristian Resources vouch for the content of these sites and numbers for the life of this study guide.

All rights reserved. No portion of this book may be reproduced, stored in a retrieval system, or transmitted in any form or by any means—electronic, mechanical, photocopy, recording, scanning, or other—except for brief quotations in critical reviews or articles, without the prior written permission of the publisher.

HarperChristian Resources titles may be purchased in bulk for church, business, fundraising, or ministry use. For information, please e-mail ResourceSpecialist@ ChurchSource.com.

First Printing August 2019 / Printed in the United States of America
23 24 25 26 27 LBC 36 35 34 33 32

CONTENTS

Why We Need the Holy Spirit

As Christians, we have each had an experience with the Holy Spirit—otherwise, we wouldn't be Christians. But many believers today have been taught erroneously about the Holy Spirit. I know people who have taken one verse out of the Bible and built an entire theology of the Holy Spirit on it. For a proper understanding of who the Holy Spirit is and how He works in our lives, we must have the *whole counsel* of God's Word on the subject.

As in all areas of study, we err if we base our believing on just one isolated concept. Truth in God's Word is expressed repeatedly. Verses build on verses to create the whole meaning of God's message to us. Our perspective is limited, and in error, unless we take in the whole of God's truth. This is the goal of the study you are holding in your hands—to explore what the Bible says about the Holy Spirit so we can have a fuller experience with Him.

This book can be used by you alone or by several people in a small-group study. At various times, you will be asked to relate to the material in one of the following four ways.

First, what new insights have you gained? Make notes about the insights you have. You may want to record them in your Bible or in a separate journal. As you reflect on your new understanding, you are likely to see how God has moved in your life.

Second, have you ever had a similar experience? You approach the Bible from your own unique background . . . your own particular set of understandings about the world that you bring with you when you open God's Word. For this reason, it is important to consider how your experiences are shaping your understanding and allow yourself to be open to the truth that God reveals.

Third, how do you feel about the material? While you should not depend solely on your emotions as a gauge for your faith, it is important for you to be aware of them as you study a passage of Scripture and can freely express them to God. Sometimes, the Holy Spirit will use your emotions to compel you to look at your life in a different or challenging way.

Fourth, in what way do you feel challenged to respond or to act? God's Word may inspire you or challenge you to take a particular action. Take this challenge seriously and find ways to move into it. If God reveals a particular need that He wants you to address, take that as His "marching orders." God will empower you to do something with the challenge that He has just given you.

Start your Bible study sessions in prayer. Ask God to give you spiritual eyes to see and spiritual ears to hear. As you conclude your study, ask the Lord to seal what you have learned so you will not forget it. Ask Him to help you grow into the fullness of the nature and character of Christ Jesus.

I encourage you to keep the Bible at the center of your study. A genuine Bible study stays focused on God's Word and promotes a growing faith and a closer walk with the Holy Spirit in each person who participates.

THE SPIRIT-FILLED LIFE IS FOR EVERY BELIEVER

IN THIS LESSON

Learning: What does the phrase "Spirit-filled life" actually mean?

Growing: Who can have a Spirit-filled life?

In all likelihood, the words "Spirit-filled life" evoke one of three responses in you. You may say, "I don't know what you're talking about." If this is your response, you are not alone. Many people don't know much about the Holy Spirit . . . and they know even less about how He works in the life of every Christian.

You may say, "I'm not sure I want anything to do with the Holy Spirit. Everything I've heard about the Him seems too divisive or too emotional for me." If that's your response, I have encouragement for you. If you are a born-again Christian, you already have a relationship with the Holy Spirit, whether you have acknowledged Him or not! Furthermore, He is not divisive or invasive. People may be . . . but He is not.

You may say, "Oh, yes! The Spirit-filled life is the most wonderful life a person can know. I wouldn't trade the Spirit-filled life for all the riches in the world or for any other experience!" If that's your response, I say *amen*—so be it. The Spirit-filled life is the only way for a Christian to experience all that God wants us to be, say, and do. It is life to the fullest . . . the true abundant life that Jesus promised. As He said to His disciples, "I have come that they may have life, and that they may have it more abundantly" (John 10:10).

The Spirit-filled life is not based on emotions, though you are likely to feel various emotions as the Holy Spirit works in you to produce the character of Christ and to replicate the ministry of Christ in your life and the world. A believer may feel the Holy Spirit in one time and place but not in another time and place . . . but this is simply due to the capricious nature of human emotions. Feelings rise and fall, come and go—but the Holy Spirit does not. If you have accepted Jesus Christ as your Lord and Savior, your salvation was sealed forever by the Holy Spirit at the moment you confessed your sins and received God's forgiveness.

The Spirit-filled life is marked by purpose, power, and effectiveness. It is not something you can study from afar—it is to be *experienced*. It is lived out in real life and involves facing real—and sometimes difficult—circumstances and situations. In the end, the Spirit-filled life is not something you *do* but something you *have* because of who is living and working inside you. God wants each of His children to live a Spirit-filled life, and He expects you to be led by the Spirit each day.

1. "Then Peter said to them, 'Repent, and let every one of you be baptized in the name of Jesus Christ for the remission of sins; and you shall receive the gift of the Holy Spirit. For the promise is to you and to your children, and to all who are afar off, as many as the

Lord our God will call'" (Acts 2:38–39). Why does Peter refer to the Holy Spirit as a "gift"? What does this teach about His character? His availability?

....

....

....

....

....

....

....

....

....

2. According to the apostle Peter's words in this passage, what is required of a person to receive the Holy Spirit and start living a Spirit-filled life?

....

....

....

....

....

....

....

....

OUR NEED FOR THE HOLY SPIRIT

Most of us have no difficulty admitting, "I need God the Father in my life." We recognize God the Father as our all-powerful, ever-present, and holy Creator. In a similar way, most of us have no difficulty admitting, "I need Jesus Christ in my life." We recognize we are sinful creatures by nature and must have the all-sufficient atonement made possible by Christ Jesus on the cross if we are to experience forgiveness for our sins and receive eternal life. We understand He came into the world so we might be restored to a full relationship with our heavenly Father, who desires to bless us as His children. In many ways, we need Christ Jesus in our lives because of our need for a relationship with the Father. But do we need the Holy Spirit?

To answer this question, we need to recognize the Holy Spirit is part of the holy Trinity—Father, Son, *and* Holy Spirit. You need Him just as much as you need the Father and the Son. In fact, the Holy Spirit makes possible your growth as a believer and enables you to experience a deepening fellowship with Jesus and the Father. You need Him at work in you if you are to fulfill your earthly destiny in Christ and become the person the Father created you to be.

Think of this in terms of driving your car. When you get into your automobile, what is the first thing you should do? You may say "pray"—and I would not disagree with that response. But I have in mind something physical that you should do before you release the parking brake, put the car in gear, and hit the gas pedal to accelerate down the road. The first thing you should do when you get into your car is fasten your seatbelt.

Now, *why* do you fasten your seatbelt? Do you do this because you are expecting to get into an accident? No, the reason you choose to put on your seatbelt—besides the fact that it is the law in most places—is so you will be safe just *in case* you get into an accident. In the same way, when you and I get up in the morning to start our day, one of the first things we should be doing is seeking the guidance of the Holy Spirit in our lives. We need to ask the Holy Spirit to direct us in every situation we face. Before we make a decision about anything, or when we meet with someone, or when we formulate a response when someone asks us a question, we want the Holy Spirit to speak into our hearts. We *need* the Holy Spirit's continual involvement.

3. The Holy Spirit is part of the Trinity—Father, Son, *and* Holy Spirit. Given this, why do you think He is often the most misunderstood member of the Trinity? What are some questions you have had in the past concerning His role in your life?

....

....

....

....

....

....

4. "I will give you a new heart and put a new spirit within you; I will take the heart of stone out of your flesh and give you a heart of flesh. I will put My Spirit within you and cause you to walk in My statutes, and you will keep My judgments and do them" (Ezekiel 36:26–27). What does this passage say about the role of the Holy Spirit in your life?

....

....

....

....

....

....

THE HOLY SPIRIT'S PRESENCE FROM THE BEGINNING

As we think about the Holy Spirit, we need to remember He has been a part of the Trinity from the beginning. In Genesis 1:1–2 we read, "In the beginning God created the heavens and the earth. The earth was without form, and void; darkness was on the face of the deep. And the Spirit of God was hovering over the face of the waters." Later, when we read of the creation of Adam, we find the Lord stating, "Let Us make man in Our image, according to Our likeness" (Genesis 1:26). The Holy Spirit, as part of the Trinity, was present and active in Creation.

As we progress through the Old Testament, we find repeated mentions of the Holy Spirit and His empowerment of people to perform certain tasks. In each Old Testament instance, the Spirit of the Lord came upon certain people to help them fulfill leadership roles—to help them carry out God's plan and purpose among His people. The Holy Spirit helped them in a wide variety of ways, enabling and equipping them to do what God had called them to do in their roles as artisans, judges, warriors, prophets, and kings.

In some cases, the Holy Spirit came a person so he or she could prophesy or speak in the name of the Lord. One individual was Isaiah, who wrote, "The Spirit of the Lord GOD is upon Me, because the Lord has anointed Me to preach good tidings to the poor" (Isaiah 61:1). Likewise, Ezekiel speaks about an indwelling of the Spirit that allows him to prophesy and speak God's word to the people: "And He said to me, 'Son of man, stand on your feet, and I will speak to you.' Then the Spirit entered me when He spoke to me, and set me on my feet; and I heard Him who spoke to me" (Ezekiel 2:1-2).

In each case, we find the Holy Spirit came to individuals in the Old Testament to help them with specific works or ministries—and then He departed from them. At that time, the Holy Spirit did not come to stay in the lives of men and women. That was simply not the pattern we find in the stories told in the Old Testament. But in the New Testament, as we will discuss further in a later lesson, we find Jesus promising His disciples the Holy Spirit would indwell them and become a continual source of divine assistance in their lives.

Now, this is not to say the Holy Spirit works in the Old Testament in a manner that is *contradictory* to the manner in which He works in the New Testament. Certainly, the Holy Spirit works in the New Testament by providing leadership assistance and also by giving clear words of direction and truth. The difference is that the Spirit did not *abide* continually with the people in the Old Testament. This is particularly evident in the life of Saul, whom Samuel anointed to be the first king of Israel. Early in his rule, we read of Saul encountering a group of prophets, and "the Spirit of God came upon him, and he prophesied among them" (1 Samuel 10:10). But later, after Saul disobeyed God and David was anointed king, we read that the "the Spirit of the LORD departed from Saul" (1 Samuel 16:14).

So it was that when Jesus came into the world, the masses of people who lived in Israel at the time had no experience with the ongoing presence of the Holy Spirit. And we have no mention in the Old Testament of the Holy Spirit coming to all the children of Israel at any time. But that would all change in the New Testament with Jesus' promise to send the Holy Spirit . . . and His arrival in the lives of the disciples who gathered in the upper room on the day of Pentecost.

5. "See, I have called by name Bezalel the son of Uri, the son of Hur, of the tribe of Judah. And I have filled him with the Spirit of God, in wisdom, in understanding, in knowledge, and in all manner of workmanship, to design artistic works, to work in gold, in silver, in bronze, in cutting jewels for setting, in carving wood, and to work in all manner of workmanship" (Exodus 31:2–5). The Lord sent His Spirit to Bezalel when the Israelites were commanded to construct the tabernacle. Why did Bezalel need the Holy Spirit?

6. What does this reveal to us about the Holy Spirit's role in the Old Testament?

....

....

....

....

....

7. Why did the Holy Spirit come upon certain people in Old Testament times? Why was it necessary for Christ to pay the price of sin on the cross before the Holy Spirit could indwell *all* of God's people?

....

....

....

....

....

....

BEYOND ADEQUATE

The truth of the matter is that today, many Christians do not understand the role of the Holy Spirit in their lives, do not consider Him as an active member of the Trinity, and do not feel compelled to lead more than just an *adequate* Christian life. They believe that if they go to church, read their Bible occasionally, and say their prayers once in a while, they are going to be all right with God. Occasionally, they may volunteer to serve others in a particular way—perhaps as an usher, or as a member of a church committee, or as a host for a small group, or as a member of an evangelism team—and they consider that ministry as above the norm.

But let me challenge you today. God doesn't call you (or anyone) to just an adequate Christian life. He wants to have a daily walking-and-talking relationship with you in which you experience His presence, trust Him for wisdom, drawn on His strength, and rely on Him for results—at every step you take, every decision you make, every conversation you have, and every thought you think. The Lord desires to live within you. He desires to communicate to you and through you. He desires to live out His life through your expression of it—a perfect blending of His perfection and your unique talents, traits, and personality.

There is no such thing as an average Christian life. Either you are living a vibrant Spirit-filled life . . . or you aren't. You are either in forward motion or in a pause position. You are either living in the fullness of the Holy Spirit or you aren't. So make a decision today to choose the Spirit-filled life. God will not force Himself on you or force Himself to operate within you. He works by invitation only. He won't overstep the boundaries of your will.

As you begin this study, you probably have some preconceptions about the Holy Spirit and how He works within a person's life. I encourage you to lay them aside and approach these lessons with a wide-open heart and mind. You can learn and experience something here—but only if you are willing to be changed in your inner person.

8. "Now may the God of hope fill you with all joy and peace in believing, that you may abound in hope by the power of the Holy Spirit" (Romans 15:13). How does the Holy Spirit enable you to lead a vibrant hope-filled life?

9. "But the Helper, the Holy Spirit, whom the Father will send in My name, He will teach you all things, and bring to your remembrance all things that I said to you" (John 14:26). When you hear the phrase "Spirit-filled life," what comes to your mind?

....

....

....

....

....

....

10. Are you open to experiencing more of the Holy Spirit in your life? Do you want more out of your relationship with Christ Jesus than you are currently experiencing? Explain.

....

....

....

....

....

TODAY AND TOMORROW

Today: I recognize that the Holy Spirit dwells within the life of every Christian.

Tomorrow: I will study the Scriptures this week to learn more about the Holy Spirit.

CLOSING PRAYER

Lord Jesus, what a wonder You are—and what a wonder it is that You gave us in the Holy Spirit, who seals us as Your purchased possession. Today, we pray that You would help us to understand the role of the Holy Spirit in our lives. Let the truths of Your Word echo in our minds and our hearts and our spirits for days to come. We desire to live the Spirit-filled life and receive all the fullness of joy that You intend for us to receive. Be alive and real to us today as we receive Your truths. In Your name we pray. Amen.

NOTES AND
PRAYER REQUESTS

· ·

Use this space to write any key points, questions, or prayer requests
from this week's study.

WHO EXACTLY IS THE HOLY SPIRIT?

— IN THIS LESSON —

Learning: Is the Holy Spirit a person or some other entity?

Growing: If the Holy Spirit is a person, then what does that mean to me?

Have you ever seen children stare in wide-eyed wonder as they listen to a story? That is the way many people are when it comes to the Holy Spirit. They don't have a clue as to His true identity or how He works in their lives. The Holy Spirit is a mystery to them.

Wide-eyed wonder is not a bad response to have to the Holy Spirit. Certainly, the Holy Spirit should inspire our awe, our wonder, and our adoration. But He does not want to be a puzzle to us. He desires to reveal Himself to us and to be known by us. Who, then, is the Holy Spirit? This is the focus of this lesson.

THE HOLY SPIRIT IS A PERSON

I believe that one of the keys to our understanding about the Holy Spirit lies in our recognition that the Holy Spirit is not an *it*—He is a person. Have you ever been asked, "Are you filled with the Holy Spirit? Do you have the Holy Spirit?" There is only one set of answers: *yes* or *no*. You can't have a little bit of the Holy Spirit. Either you have been filled by Him, or you haven't. You can't have had Him once but not have Him now. Either you have Him, or you've never had Him.

The error tends to come because we think of the Holy Spirit as a force, a power, an event, an experience, or a manifestation. I once had this exact view of the Holy Spirit. When I went to college to prepare for the ministry, the subject of the Holy Spirit came up in conversation. I must have referred to the Holy Spirit as *it*, because at the end of that discussion, one man in the group asked if I would meet with him later in his dorm room. He was a graduate student in theology, so I was honored at the invitation and gladly accepted.

When I went to his room, I was amazed to find the walls were lined entirely with books. I felt I was in the presence of a true scholar. He handed me a Greek New Testament, and I have to say that I was dismayed. I admitted to him that I had been at the college only a couple of weeks and scarcely knew more than a few words and phrases in Greek. My statement didn't deter him. He proceeded to go through the New Testament with me, one verse after another, teaching me the Holy Spirit is not an *it* but a *He*—a person, a member of the holy Trinity. My entire perspective changed.

When we begin to see the Holy Spirit as a person—not as a power or an experience—we have a much different perspective on receiving the Holy Spirit. So, from where does our false understanding of the Holy Spirit being an *it* originate? In many cases, I think it can be traced to Acts 2, where we read about the coming of the Holy Spirit into the lives of the first Christians:

When the Day of Pentecost had fully come, they were all with one accord in one place. And suddenly there came a sound from heaven, as of a rushing mighty wind, and it filled the whole house where they were sitting. Then there appeared to them divided tongues, as of fire, and one sat upon each of them. And they were all filled with the Holy Spirit and began to speak with other tongues, as the Spirit gave them utterance (Acts 2:1–4).

People tend to confuse the sights and sounds present at the Holy Spirit's arrival with the Holy Spirit Himself. They read of a rushing wind-like sound from heaven. They read of a mass of fire that seems to divide into tongues that touch each person. They read of the people speaking in languages they didn't learn, and they assume the sound, the fire, and the unknown tongues are the Holy Spirit.

However, these are manifestations of the Holy Spirit's coming to the church on the day of Pentecost shortly after Jesus' ascension. They do *not* represent the Holy Spirit Himself. The sound is *as* a rushing mighty wind. The glowing light seems *as* divided tongues of fire. The Holy Spirit is infinitely more than any single manifestation of His presence.

1. Why were the disciples "all with one accord in one place" when the Holy Spirit came to them? What does this suggest about the Holy Spirit's role in the church?

2. Consider each of the manifestations of the Spirit's presence: wind, tongues of fire, and speaking in foreign languages. What does each reveal about the Holy Spirit?

....

....

....

....

....

....

THE HOLY SPIRIT IS PART OF THE TRINITY

What makes a human being different from any of God's other creatures? The three foremost qualities of humanity are these:

- *Knowledge*—an ability to know, understand, recognize, and have meaning.
- *Will*—an ability to make choices and decisions on the basis of what one chooses to do, not as an instinctive response to external stimuli.
- *Emotion*—an ability to feel, to have feelings, and to be aware of them.

We read about the *knowing* ability of the Holy Spirit in 1 Corinthians 2:11: "For what man knows the things of a man except the spirit of the man which is in him? Even so no one knows the things of God except the Spirit of God." We read about the *will* of the Holy Spirit in 1 Corinthians 12:11: "But one and the same Spirit works all these things, distributing to each one individually as He wills" (1 Corinthians 12:11). And we read about the *emotion* of the Holy Spirit in Ephesians 4:30, where Paul admonishes, "Do not grieve the Holy

Spirit of God." We can't grieve Somebody who doesn't love us and have feelings that can be hurt. We can grieve the Holy Spirit because He has an emotional capacity. Yes, the Holy Spirit has *emotions*.

As stated in the previous lesson, the Bible reveals the Holy Spirit is the third member of the triune Godhead: God the Father, God the Son, and God the Holy Spirit. He is inseparable from the Father and the Son—He is of one nature, character, and identity with them. At the same time, He is a unique person. He has a specific identity and function, just as Jesus has a specific identity and function and the Father has a specific identity and function.

The Holy Spirit is present whenever the Father and the Son are present, and they are present whenever the Holy Spirit is present. The Holy Spirit was present at creation and was also vital in the creation of humankind: "Let Us make man in Our image, according to Our likeness" (Genesis 1:26). We have been created in the full image of God the Father, God the Son, and God the Holy Spirit. To be created in God's image means He has given us His qualities: we have an ability to know things and remember them, experience emotions and respond to life with a full range of feelings, make choices and decisions, solve problems, and have "dominion" or authority over creation. We also have God's ability to help, teach, testify, call to remembrance, and give convincing arguments.

God has created us with the full capacity to be people. As part of our creation, God "breathed" Himself into us. We have the specific ability to know God, to sense Him at work in us, and to respond to Him. He made us with the capacity to be His children and to invite Him into our lives. The Holy Spirit is the Spirit of God, and we are wise to refer to Him in that way:

- The Holy Spirit of God almighty
- The Holy Spirit of Christ Jesus—the same Spirit who indwelled Christ
- The Holy Spirit who indwells us today

All are one and the same Holy Spirit! His role in the Trinity is to fill, energize, empower, compel behavior, produce qualities of character, and work in and through God's creation. He is not the Creator, but there is no creation without Him. He is not the Father, but there is no confirmation of our relationship with the Father without Him. He is not the entire summation of God almighty, but there is no expression of God's will apart from Him. He is not the Son, but there is no awareness of sin and no saving knowledge of Jesus Christ apart from Him. He is not Jesus, but Jesus did not do anything apart from the Holy Spirit's empowerment.

The Holy Spirit is inseparable from Christ Jesus and from God the Father.

3. "I will pray the Father, and He will give you another Helper, that He may abide with you forever—the Spirit of truth, whom the world cannot receive, because it neither sees Him nor knows Him; but you know Him, for He dwells with you and will be in you" (John 14:16–17). What words in these verses point to the fact the Holy Spirit is a divine person? What does Jesus say are the roles of the Holy Spirit?

....

....

....

....

....

....

....

....

....

....

4. "But when the Helper comes, whom I shall send to you from the Father, the Spirit of truth who proceeds from the Father, He will

testify of Me" (John 15:26). What does this verse reveal about the triune Godhead—Father, Son, and Holy Spirit?

....

....

....

....

....

....

5. Why is it important to understand the Holy Spirit is part of the Trinity of God?

....

....

....

....

....

....

....

THE HOLY SPIRIT IS GOD'S PROMISE TO THE BELIEVER

The Holy Spirit has a unique relationship with believers. The Bible states that if you have Christ, you have the Holy Spirit of God. He is the seal of your commitment to Jesus. In other words, when you accept Jesus Christ as the atonement for your sins, the Holy Spirit automatically seals that decision before the Father in heaven. You belong to God forever. There is no unsealing of what the Holy Spirit seals— not by your actions or by the actions of any other person.

Conversely, if you do not have the Holy Spirit living in you, you haven't received Jesus Christ as your Savior. He is God's seal and guarantee on your life—He is proof of God's claim that you belong to Him. A person cannot be a Christian and not have the Holy Spirit within.

Some people ask, "Have you received the Holy Spirit since you became a Christian?" This question is an impossibility. You received the Holy Spirit *as part of your receiving Christ*. You can't receive just one part of the Trinity. When you became a Christian—when you confessed your sins and asked for God's forgiveness—you received the Holy Spirit. The Spirit of God came and indwelled your spirit and claimed you as His own. He has put you into full relationship with the Father and the Son, because He is inseparable from the Father and the Son. He now works to live His life—the same quality of life that Jesus Christ lived—in you and through you.

Jesus promised the Holy Spirit to His disciples, and that promise extends to you as His disciple today. Jesus said, "But the Helper, the Holy Spirit, whom the Father will send in My name, He will teach you all things" (John 14:26). Jesus said the Father *will* send the Spirit. At the time of Jesus' ascension, He said to His disciples, "Behold, I send the Promise of My Father upon you; but tarry in the city of Jerusalem until you are endued with power from on high" (Luke 24:49). It was the promise that Jesus had made to them on the night of the Last Supper—the promise of the Holy Spirit's coming to them to help and comfort them in His absence.

In Acts 1:8, Jesus made this additional statement at the time of His ascension: "You shall receive power *when* the Holy Spirit has come upon you; and you shall be witnesses to Me in Jerusalem, and in all Judea and Samaria, and to the end of the earth" (emphasis added). There was no doubt in His mind it would happen for those who followed Him.

On the day of Pentecost, Peter described the events that had transpired as follows: "This Jesus God has raised up, of which we are all witnesses. Therefore being exalted to the right hand of God, and having received from the Father the promise of the Holy Spirit,

He poured out this which you now see and hear" (Acts 2:32–33). Peter was saying, "We received the One who was promised. You witnessed the manifestation of His presence coming into our lives with your own eyes and ears." The Holy Spirit is God's promise to you as His child today. If you are a follower of the Lord Jesus Christ, you have the Holy Spirit living in you.

6. Have you accepted Jesus Christ as your Savior? If not, what is preventing you from making this decision?

....

....

....

....

....

....

7. If you are a Christian, how do you know for sure the Holy Spirit is within you?

....

....

....

....

....

The Holy Spirit Is the Power of the Believer

Jesus promised the Holy Spirit to those who followed Him because He knew they would need the Holy Spirit in them if they were to be faithful, steadfast, and effective in their walk with God. The Holy Spirit enables people to live the Christian life.

In Ephesians 1:19–21, Paul prayed the believers would know "the exceeding greatness of [God's] power toward us who believe, according to the working of His mighty power which He worked in Christ when He raised Him from the dead and seated Him at His right hand in the heavenly places, far above all principality and power and might and dominion."

Paul wanted the believers in Ephesus to know they had full resurrection power in their lives. They had the same power that raised Christ Jesus from the dead. Certainly, such power was able to raise them from their sins. Not only that, but the power was above any other principality, power, dominion, or might. Nothing is more powerful than the Holy Spirit in you.

8. "Now to Him who is able to do exceedingly abundantly above all that we ask or think, according to the power that works in us, to Him be glory in the church by Christ Jesus to all generations, forever and ever. Amen" (Ephesians 3:20–21). According to these verses, what is the Holy Spirit able to do in your life?

....

....

....

....

....

9. What is the "power that works in us"? What does this power accomplish?

....

....

....

....

....

10. How do you respond to the fact that you have access to the same power that raised Jesus from the dead? How has that truth impacted your life?

....

....

....

....

....

....

TODAY AND TOMORROW

Today: The Holy Spirit is part of the Trinity of God, and He brings God's power to my life.

Tomorrow: I will spend time this week studying what the Bible teaches concerning the Spirit's power in my life.

CLOSING PRAYER

Holy Spirit, thank You for the promise that if we have Christ, we have You living within our hearts. Thank You for representing the seal of our commitment to Jesus. We know that we belong to God and there is no unsealing of what You have sealed. Help us to remain strong against our enemy, the devil, and to not listen to his lies. Help us to understand the work You want to do in our hearts so we can live the life Jesus wants us to have to the fullest.

NOTES AND PRAYER REQUESTS

Use this space to write any key points, questions, or prayer requests from this week's study.

RELYING ON THE HOLY SPIRIT'S POWER IN US

Learning: What does the Holy Spirit do for a Christian?

Growing: How am I to respond to the Holy Spirit's presence in my life?

The writers of the New Testament described the power of the Holy Spirit power in Christians by the Greek word *dunamis*, from which we get the English word *dynamite*. The Holy Spirit causes things to happen! His power is infinite power and blasts the sin out of our lives. In this lesson, we will examine the characteristics of this power of the Holy Spirit within us.

THE HOLY SPIRIT PURIFIES US

First and foremost, the power of the Holy Spirit purifies us. In the New Testament, the nature of the Holy Spirit is often identified with fire.

We see this in Acts 2:3, where Luke portrays the Holy Spirit's manifestation as "divided tongues, as of fire." Fire, or intense temperature, is used to melt and purify metals. This image appears in the Old Testament and applies to all God's people. In Isaiah 1:25, God says, "I will . . . thoroughly purge away your dross, and take away all your alloy." This same imagery can be applied to God's purification of all that makes us impure before the Father. The Holy Spirit burns sin out of us so we won't burn in our sin.

Paul wrote to the Romans, "If Christ is in you, the body is dead because of sin, but the Spirit is life because of righteousness. But if the Spirit of Him who raised Jesus from the dead dwells in you, He who raised Christ from the dead will also give life to your mortal bodies through His Spirit who dwells in you" (Romans 8:10-11). The Holy Spirit burns sin from us, and He cleanses the fleshly nature so we no longer desire to sin. In other words, once He has purified us, part of that purification process is a desire within us to remain pure.

Fire and burning are not comfortable images to us. Fire sounds painful—and sometimes the fire of the Holy Spirit in our lives *is* painful. His chastisement and admonishment often go against what we desire in our human nature. But the results of His purification process are glorious! As the Lord purifies us, we are made acceptable in His sight and are made ready for use in His kingdom. Purification is a necessary part of being *sanctified*, which means to be cleansed and set aside as holy in God's eyes.

It is vital for us to understand that purity of heart cannot be separated from the power of the Holy Spirit. We are purified by the Holy Spirit, and we continue to walk in purity because of His presence and power within us. Many people attempt to clean up their lives by changing their behavior. They start going to church, attending a Bible study, giving some of their money to God, reading their Bibles, and saying their prayers. None of these actions can drive sin from our lives. Only as we yield to the Holy Spirit can we be completely cleansed.

1. "Looking for the blessed hope and glorious appearing of our great God and Savior Jesus Christ, who gave Himself for us, that He might redeem us from every lawless deed and purify for Himself His own special people, zealous for good works" (Titus 2:13–14). What does it mean to be "zealous for good works"? Give practical examples.

....

....

....

....

....

....

2. How does the Holy Spirit "redeem us from every lawless deed"? How has the Holy Spirit worked in your life to refine your character? Give practical examples.

....

....

....

....

....

....

3. When have you found the Holy Spirit's purifying process to be painful? In what areas have you seen true change? How was the change worth the temporary discomfort?

....

....

....

....

....

....

THE HOLY SPIRIT CONVICTS US

The Holy Spirit also convicts us of our sin. Before we can be cleansed of our wrongdoing, we must first be convinced that we *have* sinned. This is part of the Holy Spirit's purification process in us. Paul wrote about this to the Corinthians when he asked them, "Do you not know that you are the temple of God and that the Spirit of God dwells in you? If anyone defiles the temple of God, God will destroy him. For the temple of God is holy, which temple you are" (1 Corinthians 3:16–17).

No believer in Christ would think of defacing or destroying a church building. We consider our churches to be sacred places. In like manner, Paul taught the Corinthians their bodies were sacred places. Their bodies were indwelled by God's Holy Spirit, just as the temple of old was filled with God's Holy Spirit. In other words, the Corinthians had no right to themselves any longer. They belonged to God. They were His possessions.

The Holy Spirit will not allow anything that is not holy, pure, and righteous to coexist with Him in His temple. For that reason, the Holy Spirit continually seeks to convict us when we sin. We may turn a deaf ear to His conviction for so long that it seems it has been reduced to a whisper, but He will convict us of our sin until we confess it, repent of it, and are cleansed of it. Our sin is a stain on our purity before God, and the Holy Spirit will not allow it to stand unchallenged.

So be sensitive to the convicting power of the Holy Spirit in your life. Respond to Him with a contrite and humble heart. Face your sin. Only then can you be forgiven of it and restored to the purity necessary for the Lord to use you as He desires.

4. "When [the Holy Spirit] has come, He will convict the world of sin, and of righteousness, and of judgment" (John 16:8). Why is it important for the Holy Spirit to convict us of sin? What would happen if He didn't convict us in this manner?

....

....

....

....

....

....

5. How is the Holy Spirit necessary for us to gain righteousness?

....

....

....

....

....

....

THE HOLY SPIRIT STRENGTHENS US

The Holy Spirit imparts strength to us. Paul prayed for the Ephesians that the Lord "would grant [them], according to the riches of His glory, to be strengthened with might through His Spirit in the inner man" (Ephesians 3:16). To be made strong implies a person is initially weak by nature or has been weakened by circumstance. This is certainly true for any of us who are honest with ourselves. We struggle in staying obedient to God's Word. We are fragile in our bodies, frail in our resolve, and failing in our courage. We are weak creatures apart from the Holy Spirit.

Paul admonished the Ephesians to grow into maturity in Christ "to the measure of the stature of the fullness of Christ; that [they] should no longer be children, tossed to and fro and carried about with every wind of doctrine, by the trickery of men, in the cunning craftiness of deceitful plotting" (Ephesians 4:13-14). We are to become strong in Christ, and the only way that we can do this is through the Holy Spirit. With the Holy Spirit, we are strong, even to the point that we can "do all things through Christ" who strengthens us (Philippians 4:13).

The Spirit of Christ is the same Holy Spirit who is working in our lives. We *can* do all things that God commands us to do. We *can* live a quality of life that is the same as that lived by Christ. We *can* live a life free of sin and bold in speech and action because we are empowered by the same Holy Spirit who empowered Jesus.

Paul recited to the Corinthians a list of troubles he had experienced and then concluded, "Therefore most gladly I will rather boast in my infirmities, that the power of Christ may rest upon me. . . . For when I am weak, then I am strong" (2 Corinthians 12:9–10). Paul knew the reality of the Holy Spirit's power in his life—a power that had strengthened him to withstand all kinds of persecution, dangers, weariness, and physical deprivation. He knew the Holy Spirit had strengthened him in times when he was afflicted by a "thorn in the flesh" (2 Corinthians 12:7.) He told the Corinthians that he had learned this truth from the Lord: "My grace is sufficient for you, for My strength is made perfect in weakness" (2 Corinthians 12:9). Paul was no stranger to hardship, but he was also no stranger to God's power working in him.

The Holy Spirit revives us and gives us strength when we are weakened by disease, injury, or natural calamity. He enables us to endure pain and times of adversity. He makes us strong so we might defeat the enemy. He empowers us against Satan's *temptations* by helping us to resist impulses to sin (see 1 Corinthians 10:12–13). He empowers us against the enemy's *lies* by helping us to discern the truth and see the ploys of the devil (see John 16:13). He empowers us against *attacks* by being part of our defensive armor (see Ephesians 6:18).

The Holy Spirit strengthens us to resist the devil and defeat his influence (see James 4:7.) Satan accuses us before the Father at every turn, but God's promise is that we have the strength of the Holy Spirit to withstand the devil's activity against us, making his accusations null and void (see Revelation 12:10). The Holy Spirit is omnipotent. He has all the power we can ever need—and infinitely more. We can ask Him Spirit to impart the strength we need today.

6. "He said to me, 'My grace is sufficient for you, for My strength is made perfect in weakness.'" (2 Corinthians 12:9). What does it mean to have God's strength made perfect through your weakness? When have you seen this in your life?

....
....
....
....
....
....
....
....

7. What does it mean that God's grace is sufficient for you? When have you seen this in your life or in the life of someone you know?

....
....
....
....
....
....
....

THE HOLY SPIRIT EQUIPS US FOR MINISTRY

Finally, the Holy Spirit equips us for ministry. The Holy Spirit does His work *in* us so He can do His work *through* us. We are not indwelled by the Holy Spirit so we can have an ecstatic experience or feel peace in our relationship with God. Those emotions may arise as we experience the presence of the Holy Spirit at work, but the Holy Spirit indwells us so we might be His witnesses and do His work on this earth.

Remember Jesus' words in Acts 1:8: "You shall receive power when the Holy Spirit has come upon you; and you shall be witnesses to Me in Jerusalem, and in all Judea and Samaria, and to the end of the earth." The foremost manifestation of the Lord's presence in our lives is that we are His witnesses. Our changed lives say something to the world. We speak with our very lives the gospel of Christ. We display by our words and deeds God's power to transform people from a state of sinfulness to a state of righteousness. We are purified and strengthened so we might be living vessels of God's love and power made known to others.

In future lessons we will discuss the specific types of equipping the Lord does in our lives, but at this point we can just say that God wants to use *us*. He has a plan and a purpose for our lives. He has a role for us to fill that only we can fill. If we are to accomplish the reason for our existence, to fulfill our destiny, and to know the inner satisfaction of a mission accomplished, we must have the power of the Holy Spirit at work within us.

We cannot succeed in God's eyes without the Holy Spirit's help. If we try to do so, we will only fall short. Anything we try to do apart from the Holy Spirit's help and guidance is doomed to failure. It won't last because it has nothing of His eternal presence in it. On the other hand, everything we do in the Holy Spirit cannot help being eternal, life-giving, and a blessing to us and others. In Him, we are and have all that is necessary . . . forever.

8. "The Gentiles should be fellow heirs, of the same body, and partakers of His promise in Christ through the gospel, of which I became a minister according to the gift of the grace of God given to me by the effective working of His power" (Ephesians 3:6–7). In what ways was Paul a "minister" of God's grace to the Gentiles (and others)? In what ways can you be a minister of God's grace?

....

....

....

....

....

....

....

9. What is "the effective working" of God's power? What role does the Holy Spirit play in this process? What role do you play?

....

....

....

....

....

....

....

....

10. "Now may the God of peace Himself sanctify you completely; and may your whole spirit, soul, and body be preserved blameless at the coming of our Lord Jesus Christ. He who calls you is faithful, who also will do it" (1 Thessalonians 5:23–24). What does it mean to be *sanctified* completely? Why does Paul include spirit, soul, and body in this promise?

....

....

....

....

....

All that the Holy Spirit is He makes available to you so you might help, teach, guide, speak words of conviction, and call God's truth to the remembrance of others. He has all knowledge—He gives you His wisdom so you might make good decisions and sound judgments. He has capacity for all emotion—He imparts to you His great heart so you might love others with an expanded ability. He operates out of His will—He imparts to you a knowledge of His will so you might move in strength and obedience, and avoid the pitfalls of sin.

So today, ask the Holy Spirit how He desires you to give testimony to His presence in your life. Ask Him in what areas you need to let His witness shine brighter through you. And remember . . . what He calls you to do, He also equips you to do.

TODAY AND TOMORROW

Today: The Holy Spirit gives me everything I need to purify my life and conquer the enemy.

Tomorrow: I will ask the Lord this week to show me areas in my life that need to be purified.

CLOSING PRAYER

· ·

Holy Spirit, thank You for purifying us. Although the process is painful, we know the result will make us pleasing in God's sight and ready for His use. Thank You for convicting us. We accept that You will not allow anything that is unrighteous to coexist with You in Your temple, and we want to be cleansed of our sins so we can lead effective lives. And thank You for strengthening us. We acknowledge that You have all the power we will never need—and we ask that You impart that strength to us today as we battle against temptations and the enemy of our soul.

NOTES AND
PRAYER REQUESTS

· ·

Use this space to write any key points, questions, or prayer requests from this week's study.

RELYING ON THE HOLY SPIRIT'S PRESENCE

IN THIS LESSON

Learning: Does the Holy Spirit ever abandon a Christian?

Growing: How does the Holy Spirit make me more like Jesus?

Sometimes, people speak of a "filling" and then a "refilling" of the Holy Spirit in a person's life. Let me assure you—based on God's Word, when the Holy Spirit indwells you, He abides with you *forever*. He does not come and go. He is with you . . . from now into eternity.

In the Gospels, Jesus refers to the Holy Spirit as *living water*. We see this in an encounter He had with a Samaritan woman one day at a well near the town of Sychar. During the conversation, Jesus said, "If you knew the gift of God, and who it is who says to you, 'Give Me a drink,' you would have asked Him, and He would have given you living water" (John 4:10). When the woman questioned the nature of this living water, Jesus said, "Whoever drinks of the water that I shall give him will never thirst. But the water that I shall give him will become in him a fountain of water springing up into everlasting life" (John 4:13–14).

Jesus later said to a multitude, "If anyone thirsts, let him come to Me and drink. He who believes in Me, as the Scripture has said, out of his heart will flow rivers of living water" (John 7:37–38). John made it clear Jesus was referring to the *Holy Spirit* as living water. He wrote, "But this He spoke concerning the Spirit, whom those believing in Him would receive; for the Holy Spirit was not yet given, because Jesus was not yet glorified" (John 7:39).

Living water refers to artesian springs—water that bubbles up through the earth in unending supply. The water from artesian springs is considered the purest water available to humankind. It flows freely without end. This is the description Jesus uses for the Holy Spirit: a freely flowing, unending, inner source of purity, strength, power, and refreshment.

1. "He who believes in Me . . . out of his heart will flow rivers of living water" (John 7:38). In what ways does the Holy Spirit's ministry resemble "living waters"?

2. What sorts of "thirst" does the Holy Spirit quench the lives of followers of Christ? When have you seen Him quench a thirst in your own life?

JESUS PROMISES TO
SEND THE HOLY SPIRIT

John says the Holy Spirit "was not yet given, because Jesus was not yet glorified" (John 7:39). He explains this further when he quotes Jesus as saying, "If you love Me, keep My commandments. And I will pray the Father, and He will give you another Helper, that He may abide with you forever—the Spirit of truth, whom the world cannot receive, because it neither sees Him nor knows Him; but you know Him, for He dwells with you and will be in you. I will not leave you orphans; I will come to you" (John 14:15–18).

Jesus was promising to send the very Spirit of God that dwelt within Him to comfort and help His disciples. He makes it plain His disciples would recognize the Holy Spirit because they had known Him as He had been manifested in Jesus. Furthermore, Jesus says the Holy Spirit will not be *with* them—which is the way they had thus far experienced the Holy Spirit in the life of Christ—but that the Holy Spirit will be *in* them.

Jesus then repeats His command for them to keep His word and explains, "If anyone loves Me, he will keep My word; and My Father will love him, and We will come to him and make Our home with him" (John 14:23). Again, we see the Holy Spirit who indwelled and worked through Jesus is the same Holy Spirit made available today to followers of Christ.

Jesus tells His disciples, "[the] Helper, the Holy Spirit, whom the Father will send in My name, He will teach you all things, and bring to your remembrance all things that I said to you" (John 14:26). He commands His disciples to abide in Him and to bear fruit (see John 15:1–10). He warns them of persecution to come and repeats His desire for them to love one another. "But when the Helper comes, whom I shall send to you from the Father, the Spirit of truth who proceeds from the Father, He will testify of Me. And you also will bear witness, because you have been with Me from the beginning" (John 15:26–27).

Again, we see the Holy Spirit comes from the Father at Jesus' request. Jesus says the Holy Spirit will testify about what He is about to do on the cross—about His becoming our all-sufficient atonement for sin. Jesus says He is telling His disciples all these things so they won't stumble. Then He says, "It is to your advantage that I go away; for if I do not go away, the Helper will not come to you; but if I depart, I will send Him to you" (John 16:7).

The disciples are puzzled about how it can be more advantageous for Jesus to be *away* from them than be *with* them. Jesus, knowing their thoughts, says, "In that day you will ask Me nothing. . . . Whatever you ask the Father in My name He will give you. Until now you have asked nothing in My name. Ask, and you will receive" (John 16:23–24).

Up to this point, the disciples had turned to Jesus for everything. They had trusted the Holy Spirit to work in Jesus to meet their needs and deliver the people. But Jesus knew that after His death, resurrection, and ascension, the disciples would no longer be present with them in bodily form. But they *would* have the Holy Spirit living inside them. They could ask the Father in Jesus' name to meet their needs, and the Holy Spirit would work through them directly. This is why Jesus said His going away was to their advantage. They would have the unlimited Holy Spirit of Christ available to them. However, Jesus could not send the Holy Spirit to His disciples until He had gone away.

As Jesus was about to ascend to His Father, He gathered His disciples together for one last word. We read, "He commanded them not to depart from Jerusalem, but to wait for the Promise of the Father, 'which,' He said, 'you have heard from Me; for John truly baptized with water, but you shall be baptized with the Holy Spirit not many days from now'" (Acts 1:4–5).

Jesus promised the Holy Spirit would come *after* He had been glorified (through His death, resurrection, and ascension). He said the Holy Spirit would be *in* His disciples. And He said the Holy Spirit would be in them as living water—a continually available source of divine assistance. Jesus said nothing of the Holy Spirit departing from His disciples at any time.

3. Why is it beneficial to have the Holy Spirit dwelling in you? Why did Jesus need to ascend to heaven for this to take place?

....

....

....

....

....

....

4. "The Spirit of truth . . . will guide you into all truth; for He will not speak on His own authority, but whatever He hears He will speak; and He will tell you things to come" (John 16:13). What does it mean that the Holy Spirit will not speak on His own authority? What does the Holy Spirit speak to us?

....

....

....

....

....

....

THE HOLY SPIRIT IN JESUS' BIRTH

There are several instances in the Gospels in which the Holy Spirit was at work in the lives of individuals. Elizabeth had an experience with the Holy Spirit when Mary came to her house and she heard Mary's greeting. Elizabeth's baby, John the Baptist, leaped in her womb, and Elizabeth "was filled with the Holy Spirit." She then prophesied to Mary, "Blessed are you among women, and blessed is the fruit of your womb!" (Luke 1:42).

Zacharias, Elizabeth's husband, was struck speechless for doubting that Elizabeth might conceive John the Baptist in her old age. After Zacharias declared their baby's name was to be John, "Zacharias was filled with the Holy Spirit," and he then prophesied about the ministry that his son would have as the "prophet of the Highest" (Luke 1:67, 76.)

We also read in Luke's Gospel, "There was a man in Jerusalem whose name was Simeon, and this man was just and devout, waiting for the Consolation of Israel, and the Holy Spirit was upon him. And it had been revealed to him by the Holy Spirit that he would not see death before he had seen the Lord's Christ" (Luke 2:25–26). Furthermore, Simeon was directed to go "by the Spirit into the temple" when Jesus' parents brought Him there (Luke 25:26). Simeon declared that Jesus was the long-awaited Messiah. Each person experienced a short-lived experience with the Holy Spirit. The purpose of these encounters appears to have been to proclaim the work of the Lord as it related to the life and ministry of Jesus.

But what about the Holy Spirit in the life of Jesus Himself? The Gospels reveal a different picture of the Holy Spirit at work prior to Jesus' coming into the world. First and foremost, we read that Jesus was conceived by the Holy Spirit. The angel Gabriel told Mary, "The Holy Spirit will come upon you, and the power of the Highest will overshadow you; therefore, also, that Holy One who is to be born will be called the Son of God" (Luke 1:35).

Every moment of Jesus' earthly existence was filled with the Holy Spirit. He was conceived by the Holy Spirit and had the Holy Spirit residing in Him continually from that moment onward. As Mary's son, He was human in every way. As God's Son, He was divine in every way. In coming to earth, Jesus gave up the glory He had as God the Son in heaven—though He did not give up His divinity.

5. What roles did the Holy Spirit fulfill in the events leading up to Jesus' birth? How did He impact the lives of Elizabeth, Zacharias, and Simeon?

....

....

....

....

....

....

....

6. What does it mean to be overshadowed by "the power of the Highest"? What does this teach you about the Holy Spirit's role in your life?

....

....

....

....

....

....

THE HOLY SPIRIT IN JESUS' MINISTRY

Many people erroneously conclude that Jesus received the Holy Spirit at His baptism in water. Matthew writes, "When He had been baptized, Jesus came up immediately from the water; and behold, the heavens were opened to Him, and He saw the Spirit of God descending like a dove and alighting upon Him. And suddenly a voice came from heaven, saying, 'This is My beloved Son, in whom I am well pleased'" (Matthew 3:16–17).

Jesus obeyed the Father in being baptized by John, and in the aftermath the Father revealed in a special way that Jesus' earthly ministry was to begin. The manifestation by the Holy Spirit was one of approval and of commissioning. He lighted "upon" Jesus, just as if the Father was tapping Him on the shoulder (as a king taps a knight on his shoulder with a sword). The Father declared His approval of Jesus and of the timing for His ministry to begin.

Nowhere in the Gospels do we have an account of Jesus *receiving* the gift of the Holy Spirit or of His having an ecstatic or mystical *experience* with the Spirit. We have no mention that He grew in the Holy Spirit. We know that He "increased in wisdom and stature, and in favor with God and men" (Luke 2:52), but that refers to Jesus' growth in His humanity, not in His divinity. Jesus was fully God from His birth . . . even as He was fully man. He had no need to be filled with the Spirit, as He was always filled with the Spirit.

Immediately after Jesus' baptism, the Holy Spirit led Him into the wilderness, where He was tempted by Satan. Jesus' human will was tested, and He emerged triumphant and completely in alignment with the will of the Holy Spirit of God. Jesus then "returned in the power of the Spirit to Galilee" (Luke 4:14). This does not mean that Jesus acquired the Holy Spirit in the wilderness or that He grew in the Holy Spirit while there. Jesus was already filled to complete fullness before He entered the time of temptation.

Jesus was not diminished in any way by His encounter with the devil during those forty days. The devil gave Jesus his best shots, and Jesus rebuffed every one. There was no one moment in *all of Jesus' ministry* in which He was operating in anything less than the full power of the Holy Spirit. Even at the end of His ministry, we have no mention that Jesus lost or gave up the Holy Spirit during His crucifixion—when He gave up His earthly life as a sacrifice for our sins—or at the time of His resurrection, or at the time of His ascension to the Father.

Jesus is filled with the Holy Spirit *always*. There has never been a moment throughout the ages when it has been otherwise. This permanent, unchanging presence of the Holy Spirit in Jesus' life qualifies Him as a member of the holy Trinity. He said repeatedly to His disciples that He didn't do anything He didn't see the Father doing (see John 5:19). He said that He and the Father were one (see John 10:30) and that He knew the Father just as the Father knew Him (John 10:15). Jesus' entire ministry was marked by the fullness of the Holy Spirit.

7. Why did the Holy Spirit descend "like a dove" on Jesus? What does the dove reveal about the Spirit's character? In what ways does the Holy Spirit make us more like Christ?

....

....

....

....

....

....

....

....

8. If followers of Christ have the same Holy Spirit living within them that Jesus possessed, what does this suggest about our power over temptation?

....

....

....

....

....

....

....

....

The Holy Spirit and the Birth of the Church

On the day of Pentecost (the fiftieth day after the Passover feast), Jesus sent His Spirit, the Holy Spirit, to infill His church—His body of believers—just as His earthly physical body had once been filled. All believers in Christ are now His body. As Paul writes, "For as the body is one and has many members, but all the members of that one body, being many, are one body, so also is Christ. For by one Spirit we were all baptized into one body— whether Jews or Greeks, whether slaves or free—and have all been made to drink into one Spirit" (1 Corinthians 12:12–13).

The Father extended the same Holy Spirit that resided in Jesus to infill all who believed and accepted what Jesus did on the cross. In so doing, He sealed their redemption in Christ (see Ephesians 1:13). The glorious event of the Holy Spirit coming to Jesus' disciples marks the birthday of the church. It is the beginning of a new and lasting manifestation of the Holy Spirit.

The Holy Spirit in us is the life of Christ in us. It is His Spirit, in His body—ours individually, and ours collectively, as we are connected to other believers. And just as the Holy Spirit never departed from Jesus during His life, so He never departs from us. What a marvelous blessing He has made available to us—a blessing unknown by all who lived prior to the cross!

9. What does it mean to be a member of the body of Christ?

10. What does it mean that we "have all been made to drink into one Spirit"? What does the verb *drink* suggest about the Holy Spirit's presence in our lives?

....

....

....

....

....

....

TODAY AND TOMORROW

Today: God gives His spirit to all Christians—permanently.

Tomorrow: I will praise the Father for the tremendous gift of His Holy Spirit in my life.

CLOSING PRAYER

Lord Jesus, we love You and praise You. Thank You for that wonderful promise of the Holy Spirit that You made to Your disciples. Thank You for sending Him to them—and to us—on the day of Pentecost. Thank You that the Holy Spirit actually dwells within us and is continually at work to convict us of our sins and help us to walk the path of godliness. Thank You for the gift of faith and for the gift of life everlasting. May we stay in step with the Spirit today, receive His direction, and take steps to move in the way the He compels us to go.

Notes and Prayer Requests

Use this space to write any key points, questions, or prayer requests from this week's study.

Relying on the Holy Spirit in Prayer

Learning: What is the purpose of prayer?

Growing: What if I don't know how to pray?

Do you struggle in prayer? If so, you aren't alone. Every Christian I know struggles at times in prayer. They wonder, "How should I pray for this situation or this person? What is the Father's will in this instance? How should I express myself to the Father to convey what I really mean?" At times, our emotions run too deep for words . . . and we are thus at a loss for words in prayer. At other times, we are confused by what we see as conflicting possibilities or problems. At still other times, we feel under such a heavy assault from the enemy that we seem to be fighting for our very lives—and all we can voice is a desperate cry for help!

Have you ever stopped to recognize that even Jesus, in His humanity, struggled with prayer? Jesus knew He had come to this earth to be the all-sufficient atonement for our sins. He said to His disciples during the final week of His life, "The hour has come that the Son of Man should be glorified. Most assuredly, I say to you, unless a grain of wheat falls into the ground and dies, it remains alone; but if it dies, it produces much grain. . . . Now My soul is troubled, and what shall I say? 'Father, save Me from this hour'? But for this purpose I came to this hour. 'Father, glorify Your name'" (John 12:23–24, 27–28).

Jesus, even with this knowledge and resolve, struggled in prayer. Matthew tells us that in the final hours before His betrayal, He agonized in prayer in the Garden of Gethsemane. He admitted to His disciples, "My soul is exceedingly sorrowful, even to death. Stay here and watch with Me" (Mathew 26:38). Jesus prayed that, if at all possible, He might be spared His crucifixion. Yet His ultimate prayer was, "My Father, if this cup cannot pass away from Me unless I drink it, Your will be done" (Matthew 26:42). Luke adds that Jesus was in such agony that "His sweat became like great drops of blood falling down to the ground" (Luke 22:44).

Yes, Jesus struggled with prayer. And so do we—if prayer means anything to us and we feel a burden to intercede for others. Yet we can take heart in those times of struggle. As Paul taught, "The Spirit also helps in our weaknesses. For we do not know what we should pray for as we ought, but the Spirit Himself makes intercession for us with groanings which cannot be uttered" (Romans 8:26). The Holy Spirit dwells within us to help us in our prayer lives! We can count on Him to make our prayers effective.

1. What does Paul mean when he says, "We do not know what we should pray for as we ought"? When have you felt that way?

2. What weaknesses does the Holy Spirit help with when it comes to prayer?

....

....

....

....

....

....

....

PRAYING WITHIN
THE FATHER'S WILL

Our desire as Christians must always be to pray within the Father's will. The Father's will includes all that is beneficial and good for us personally and all that is beneficial and good for all His children—simultaneously and eternally. His plan is greater than our ability to understand it. His purposes for our lives are beyond our comprehension.

Given this, how do we pray *within* the Father's will? If we are praying for unsaved people, our prayer should be for them to accept Jesus Christ as their personal Savior and to follow Him as their Lord. If we are praying for fellow believers in Christ Jesus, we can know that certain things are always within the will of the Father. We have a good model for this in Paul's letter to the Philippians, in which he records the following prayer for them:

I thank my God upon every remembrance of you, always in every prayer of mine making request for you all with joy, for your fellowship in the gospel from the first day until now, being confident of this very thing, that He who has begun a good work in you will complete it until the day of

Jesus Christ.... And this I pray, that your love may abound still more and more in knowledge and all discernment, that you may approve the things that are excellent, that you may be sincere and without offense till the day of Christ, being filled with the fruits of righteousness which are by Jesus Christ, to the glory and praise of God (Philippians 1:3–6, 9–11).

Paul's words tell us we can always pray the following things for believers at all times: (1) that Christ will complete the work in them that He has started, (2) that their love may abound, (3) that they may grow in knowledge and discernment, (4) that they may live sincere lives as they follow Christ and never bring offense to His name, (5) that they be filled with the fruits of righteousness, and (6) that their lives may bring glory and praise to God.

In Colossians, Paul provides another model prayer that we can always pray for our fellow believers in God's will:

[We] do not cease to pray for you, and to ask that you may be filled with the knowledge of His will in all wisdom and spiritual understanding; that you may walk worthy of the Lord, fully pleasing Him, being fruitful in every good work and increasing in the knowledge of God; strengthened with all might, according to His glorious power, for all patience and longsuffering with joy; giving thanks to the Father who has qualified us to be partakers of the inheritance of the saints in the light (Colossians 1:9–12).

It is God's will that our fellow believers in Christ know His will, have His wisdom, grow in spiritual understanding, walk in righteousness, bear fruit, grow in intimacy with the Lord, and be strong, patient, and joyful. I encourage you to use these prayers as your basic pattern of intercession for others.

3. Do you thank God for the Christian friends in your life? Why might this be within God's will for your prayer life?

....

....

....

....

....

....

....

4. What does it mean to be filled with knowledge of God's will, to walk worthy of the Lord, to be fruitful in every good work, and to grow in intimacy with the Lord? How can you pray each of these things over the life of another person this week?

....

....

....

....

....

....

....

....

THE HOLY SPIRIT'S GUIDANCE IN PRAYER

Our struggle to pray within the will of the Father occurs most often when we don't know *how* to pray. Several years ago, I visited a woman in the hospital. She was very ill, and she asked me to pray for her healing. I tried to pray as she requested, but I found myself praying for everything but her healing. In my spirit, I had a growing knowledge that healing was not God's plan for her. He was about to call her home. Sure enough, she died the next day.

In the difficult times when we don't know how to pray, or we find ourselves stopped from praying what we had intended to pray, Paul tells us the Holy Spirit "helps in our weaknesses" (Romans 8:26). This phrase in the Greek literally means that the Holy Spirit shares the load. He gets up under the burden we feel and helps us carry the prayer. The same Greek word is used in Luke 10:38–42, where we read that Martha was distracted from sitting at Jesus' feet because she was concerned about getting a meal on the table. She asked Jesus, "Tell [my sister] to *help* me" (Luke 10:40).

The implication in both places is that the help is practical in nature. In Martha's case, she is "worried and troubled" about serving her guests (Luke 10:41). This phrase implies she was running in circles. Isn't this the way we often feel in our prayers? We run all around the problem, hoping to corral it. But we can trust the Holy Spirit to help us in a practical way—to guide us into God's answers and solutions so we are praying in the will of the Father.

5. "We do not know what we should pray for as we ought, but the Spirit Himself makes intercession for us with groanings which cannot be uttered"(Romans 8:26). What does it mean that the Holy Spirit "makes intercession for us"?

....

....

....

....

....

....

....

....

....

6. Why does the Holy Spirit intercede "with groanings which cannot be uttered"? How is that comforting when you don't know what to pray?

....

....

....

....

....

....

....

....

....

....

THE HOLY SPIRIT UNDERSTANDS

If you want to receive the Holy Spirit's help in prayer, all you need to do is ask for it. Ask for His help *before* you pray and *while* you pray. Don't allow yourself to become discouraged. It is when you are the most discouraged about prayer that you need to keep on praying! Jesus promised that your Helper is always available and is instantly accessible. He is never out of the office when you need Him. God values your prayers—and He actually *commands* you to pray. Prayer is part of His plan for accomplishing His purposes on this earth. God Himself designed this plan for prayer, and He wants you to succeed in it.

Furthermore, you can trust that the Holy Spirit understands everything you think, feel, or experience. Paul says the Holy Spirit searches your heart and knows the mind of the Father (see Romans 8:27). He sees with absolute clarity what you need and what the Father desires to give to you. In fact, the Bible reveals the Holy Spirit understands three things simultaneously.

First, the Holy Spirit understands the situation you are facing. He sees its origins. He knows all the facets and all the details. *Second, the Holy Spirit understands your needs within the situation.* Paul wrote, "What then shall we say to these things? If God is for us, who can be against us? He who did not spare His own Son, but delivered Him up for us all, how shall He not with Him also freely give us all things?" (Romans 8:31–32). You have everything you need to do everything He has called you to do. *Third, the Holy Spirit understands the plan of God.* In 1 Corinthians 2:9–10, Paul writes, "'Eye has not seen, nor ear heard, nor have entered into the heart of man the things which God has prepared for those who love him.' But God has revealed them to us through His Spirit. For the Spirit searches all things, yes, the deep things of God."

As you pray, the Holy Spirit reveals God's plan to you. You pray for everything you can think of, and then you pause and listen for God to speak to us. You likely won't hear Him speak with an audible voice, but suddenly you will think of additional things to pray about. You pray for those things, and then you listen again. As you continue this process, you begin to receive knowledge from the Holy Spirit. You have a sense of resolution and peace. You gain a deep assurance that God is answering you and that He is in control.

At times, you may receive clear direction—you know what to do, when to take action, and how to pursue God's answer. In such instances, receive this knowledge by faith and thank the Lord for it. Express your gratitude to God and your intention to act on what the Lord has revealed. If you have misunderstood what the Lord has said, you can rest assured that He will be quick to correct you . . . if you remain open to the leading and guiding of the Holy Spirit.

As you pray, you may also find that certain ideas or words come to your mind. These may be words of Scripture, or of comfort, or a message that has meaning to your situation. These eventually form a pattern that is meaningful and represents God's answer to your need.

7. "Now we have received, not the spirit of the world, but the Spirit who is from God, that we might know the things that have been freely given to us by God" (1 Corinthians 2:12). What is "the spirit of the world"? How is it different from the Holy Spirit?

....

....

....

....

....

....

8. What things "have been freely given to us by God"? How do these gifts affect your prayer life?

....

....

....

....

....

....

THE HOLY SPIRIT'S
HELP IN INTERCESSION

Paul said the Holy Spirit "makes intercession for us with groanings which cannot be uttered" (Romans 8:26). The Holy Spirit does not carry our *words* of prayer to Jesus, who in turn presents our petitions to the Father, but carries the *meaning* of our prayers. The Holy Spirit deals with us at the deepest levels of our being, and He knows what we truly need and desire. Regardless of what we may say with our lips, the Holy Spirit knows what we mean in our hearts. He intercedes for us at that level, which is deeper than words.

The Holy Spirit then reveals the Father's response in ways we can understand, though we may not be able to express that response in words. We may know, deep within, things are going to be all right, an answer is on its way, and we can rest assured God is responding with compassion and love. This means we can never pray for the *wrong* thing. The Holy Spirit sees beyond our superficial understanding to the real issue that needs resolution. His answer to us is on the basis of our need and God's plan. Therefore, His prayer for us and His answer to us are always in keeping with the will of the Father for us.

Sometimes, the Holy Spirit will direct us to pray for others in ways we might not immediately understand. As we pray, we will feel impressed to intercede for people who are far away from us or for people we do not even know. At other times, we won't be able to get a person's name off our minds, and we will feel compelled to pray on the person's behalf.

Our heavenly Father *invites* our prayers and *uses* our prayers. Although He can certainly act without our prayers, the Bible is clear that He hasn't chosen to do. He knows that as we intercede for others, it builds up our faith in the process. We see how He answers our requests, and as a result we grow in confidence that God sees and cares about every detail of our lives. There is a great reward in cooperating with the Holy Spirit in prayer. That reward is manifested in the lives of those for whom we pray as well as in our own lives.

9. "But you, beloved, building yourselves up on your most holy faith, praying in the Holy Spirit, keep yourselves in the love of God, looking for the mercy of our Lord Jesus Christ unto eternal life" (Jude 1:20–21). What does it mean to be "building yourselves up on your most holy faith"? How is this done?

10. In light of all that we have considered in this lesson, what does it mean to be "praying in the Holy Spirit"? What does it mean to "keep yourselves in the love of God"?

....

....

....

....

....

....

TODAY AND TOMORROW

Today: The Holy Spirit keeps me in constant contact, through prayer, with the Father.

Tomorrow: I will spend extra time in prayer this week to understand the Father's will.

CLOSING PRAYER

Heavenly Father, we do not always know what to pray or how we should pray. Thank You for loving us enough to provide the Holy Spirit to us as our intercessor, who speaks to You the requests that we should—but are unable—to make. We pray that You will continually make us aware, personally, of who we have living on the inside of us and the awesome potential we have to impact the lives of others. Thank You for the power You give us through prayer.

NOTES AND
PRAYER REQUESTS

Use this space to write any key points, questions, or prayer requests from this week's study.

Avoiding Sin Against the Holy Spirit

IN THIS LESSON

Learning: How is sin against the Holy Spirit different from other sin?

Growing: Can I commit the unpardonable sin?

Have you ever sinned against the Holy Spirit? Most people recognize that it is possible to sin against God the Father and against Jesus the Son. But we can also sin against the Holy Spirit. All sins are against the Trinity. However, the New Testament describes three specific ways in which our actions can be *directly* against the Holy Spirit: (1) quenching the Holy Spirit, (2) grieving the Holy Spirit, and (3) blaspheming against the Holy Spirit. When we do these things, we short-circuit His power in our lives. In this lesson, we will take a look at each of these sins against the Holy Spirit and how we can avoid them in our Christian walk.

Quenching the Holy Spirit

Paul states directly, "Do not quench the Spirit" (1 Thessalonians 5:19). As we discussed in a previous lesson, fire has long been associated with the Holy Spirit (see Acts 2:3). Fire, in turn, is associated with cleansing, light, warmth, energy, refinement, and purifying. Appropriately, the word *quench* means "to stifle or put out." Paul is saying, "Don't put out the fire of the Holy Spirit in your life. Don't throw cold water on the fire of God in your heart."

We can never throw enough cold water on the fire of God to put it out completely. We cannot banish the Holy Spirit from our lives once we have confessed Christ. He has indwelled us and sealed our redemption. But we can impede the effectiveness of the Holy Spirit working in our lives. We can override His will, reject His promptings, or ignore His presence.

Have you ever been in the room with another person who ignored you? You might say such a person gave you the "cold shoulder." We can do this to the Holy Spirit—and in so doing, we will cut short the work He might otherwise do in us. The Holy Spirit will not move against our will or without our invitation for Him to work in us. His work in our lives is only as powerful and effective as we allow it to be. God's desire is for us to be strong in the Holy Spirit—for us to accept His work in our lives and act boldly in the fullness of His power.

There are three ways we can quench the work of the Holy Spirit. *First, we say no to something God directs us to do.* We choose our will over God's will and go our own way. The Holy Spirit can do nothing to help us and can't keep us in the center of God's plan if we turn away from His leading. He will not help us do something He knows is contrary to God's best for us.

Second, we ignore the Holy Spirit's presence. Again, this is a matter of the will. We can go about living our lives and refuse to acknowledge the Holy Spirit's help, or refuse to invite His help, or refuse to accept His help. Each of these actions quenching His work within us.

Third, we repeatedly sin. Our sin causes the Holy Spirit to convict us of our wrongdoing—and as a result of that sin, we miss out on the blessings God has for us. When we sin, we evoke the chastisement of the Holy Spirit in our lives and quench His eager desire to produce good fruit in us. He cannot reward our unfaithfulness or participate in our rebellion.

We need to consciously choose to keep our relationship kindled with the Holy Spirit in order to avoid quenching His work in this manner. Anyone who has ever camped or had a fireplace knows it is easier to keep a fire burning than it is to build one. We must maintain our relationship with the Holy Spirit. We need to talk to Him daily (just as we might pray to God the Father and Jesus the Son), recognize His presence, ask for His help, and invite Him to guide us into right paths.

When we sin, we need to be quick to respond to His convicting nudges. We should confess our sin immediately, repent of it, and turn back to the way we know God wants us to walk. When the Holy Spirit prompts us to move in a certain direction, it is important for us to say yes. We need to respond quickly to what He leads us to do and stay strong in the Lord.

1. "Therefore submit to God. Resist the devil and he will flee from you" (James 4:7). How does acknowledging the Holy Spirit and submitting to His work help us to remain strong in our faith so we can resist the attacks and schemes of the devil?

2. "Do not be deceived, God is not mocked; for whatever a man sows, that he will also reap" (Galatians 6:7). How does repeatedly sowing the "seeds" of sin quench the work of the Holy Spirit in our lives?

....
....
....
....
....
....
....

3. "Be strong in the Lord and in the power of His might" (Ephesians 6:10). What does it mean to be strong in the Lord? How can maintaining our relationship with the Holy Spirit help us to remain strong in the power of God's might?

....
....
....
....
....
....
....

GRIEVING THE HOLY SPIRIT

A second way in which we short-circuit the work of the Holy Spirit is by grieving Him. Paul wrote, "Do not grieve the Holy Spirit of God, by whom you were sealed for the day of redemption" (Ephesians 4:30). These words are embedded within a passage in which Paul admonished the believers in Ephesus to "no longer walk as the rest of the

Gentiles walk" but "put on the new man which was created according to God, in true righteousness and holiness" (Ephesians 4:17, 24). He told them to put aside lying, anger, stealing, and corrupt speech (see Ephesians 4:25–29). He summed it up by saying, "Let all bitterness, wrath, anger, clamor, and evil speaking be put away from you, with all malice. And be kind to one another, tenderhearted, forgiving one another, even as God in Christ forgave you" (Ephesians 4:31–32).

We grieve the Holy Spirit when we disobey God's commandments and when we choose to act in unrighteous ways. In other words, when we know what to do and then choose to do the opposite. The Ephesian believers knew that it was ungodly to lie, steal, be angry with one another, or speak cutting words. They knew such things gave place to the devil.

Paul lived and ministered among the Ephesians for two years, and his ministry had a powerful impact on the city of Ephesus—yet he still had to remind the Christians there not to do those things! It was as if he had to go back to square one with them. When the Ephesians broke the most obvious of God's commandments, they caused sorrow in the Holy Spirit. Paul said, in effect, "Your behavior breaks the heart of God."

The Holy Spirit can be grieved by our sins because He loves us and deeply desires to reward us, bless us, and see good fruit produced in us. He knows that sin destroys us and causes negative consequences in our lives. Just as we are grieved when we know our loved ones are doing something that will cause them harm, so He is grieved by our sinful actions.

However, we can avoid grieving the Holy Spirit by keeping God's commandments and leading a disciplined life. We can choose to immediately confess our failings when we fall into sin, repent, and then change our minds and our behaviors to conform to God's statutes. As we ask the Holy Spirit to lead us and help us on a daily basis, we can know that we have His help in our Christian walk. He keeps our footing sure. He gives us the courage to withstand temptation.

4. What are some of the ways that bitterness, wrath, anger, and speaking evil of others surface in your life? Why do these sinful actions grieve the Holy Spirit?

....

....

....

....

....

....

....

....

5. Why is it critical for believers in Christ to practice kindness and be forgiving of one another? How do these actions strengthen our relationship with the Holy Spirit?

....

....

....

....

....

....

....

....

BLASPHEMING AGAINST THE HOLY SPIRIT

In the Gospel of Matthew, we read about a confrontation between Jesus and the Pharisees, some of the religious leaders who were plotting to destroy Him because of the miracles He had performed on the Sabbath. Jesus knew what the Pharisees were plotting and what their real motivations were, but He continued His work among the people and healed a man on the Sabbath who was demon-possessed and could not see or hear.

There was no doubt the man had been healed and delivered in a powerful way. But the Pharisees were intent on destroying Jesus' credibility, so they insisted that He had healed by the power of Beelzebub, the ruler of the demons. Jesus replied, "Every kingdom divided against itself is brought to desolation" (Matthew 12:25). In other words, Satan isn't going to empower or inspire anybody to do something that is good. Satan would be setting up his own downfall.

The Pharisees were also making a statement about God—that God would not empower someone like Jesus to do good on the Sabbath. They were saying God is content to let people starve or suffer on the Sabbath—to allow them to remain demon-possessed and unable to see or hear—but the ruler of the demons, Beelzebub, is willing to see such people helped and healed. They had completely turned upside down the truth about God and the devil.

Jesus replied to them, "He who is not with Me is against Me, and he who does not gather with Me scatters abroad. . . . Every sin and blasphemy will be forgiven men, but the blasphemy against the Spirit will not be forgiven men. Anyone who speaks a word against the Son of Man, it will be forgiven him; but whoever speaks against the Holy Spirit, it will not be forgiven him, either in this age or in the age to come" (Matthew 12:30–32).

Jesus was saying, "You can say what you will about Me, but don't speak such perversion about the Holy Spirit. When you blaspheme against God in that way, you are saying that God does not desire to forgive and deliver people. And as long as you believe that and teach that to others, you won't be able to experience His forgiveness and deliverance. If you don't believe that God wants to forgive people and restore people to wholeness, you will never be open to the sacrifice that I will make on the cross of Calvary."

Jesus' words were to the Pharisees, who had put themselves into sharp conflict with Him and who were plotting His destruction. He spoke these words before His death on the cross and before His resurrection. He spoke them as a warning to the Pharisees to let them know that He knew the full intent of their hearts and the full meaning of their claims. He called this sin of blaspheming against the Holy Spirit an "unpardonable sin."

Many believers today worry they have likewise committed the unpardonable sin. But let me assure you—if you have *any* concern about having committed this kind of sin, there is *no way* that you have committed it. Furthermore, this is the *only time* we find these words in Scripture, and the message was solely directed to the Pharisees, who were cutting themselves off from the possibility of acknowledging Jesus as their Savior and Lord. At no other time in the New Testament do we find mention of an unpardonable sin. There are no warnings against it or teachings about it. To the contrary, numerous passages of Scripture announce that God's forgiveness is freely given and readily available to all for the asking.

6. "If we say that we have no sin, we deceive ourselves, and the truth is not in us. If we confess our sins, He is faithful and just to forgive us our sins and to cleanse us from all unrighteousness" (1 John 1:8–9). How do these verses prove that you cannot commit a sin God isn't willing to forgive? How does the simple act of acknowledging your sin make you eligible for forgiveness?

7. On what basis does God forgive sins? Is there anything, besides confessing, that you must do?

....

....

....

....

....

....

....

THE DANGER OF THE
UNPARDONABLE STATE

Given this evidence in the Scripture, we should not be concerned with the question of whether it is unpardonable to blaspheme against the Holy Spirit. Rather, we should focus on the more important issue: when we refuse to receive the forgiveness that God freely offers, we put ourselves into an *unpardonable state*. We can die in an unpardonable state . . . but it won't be because we have committed an unpardonable sin.

No sin is unforgivable on this side of death. But it is equally true that no sin can be forgiven on the other side of the grave. Refusing to believe in the forgiveness made available to us by the death of Christ brings about everlasting death. Accepting what Jesus did on the cross—believing in Him as Savior—brings about everlasting life.

In like manner, when we willfully turn away from God and pursue the lusts of the flesh, we tie the hands of the Holy Spirit in our lives. He will not force us to experience God's will for us. He will convict us of our sin, speak to us of Jesus, and chastise us for our rebellion, but He will not override our choices. As Christians, our rebellion will not put us into an unpardonable state—but it will put us into a miserable state!

We cannot be happy or know the fullness of God's joy, peace, and blessings if we are in sin and refuse God's forgiveness. We will be cut off from the fullness of our potential and the maximum blessing that God has for us in achieving your destiny in Him. And we will remain in that miserable state until we confess our sins to God and receive His forgiveness.

8. "To [Jesus] all the prophets witness that, through His name, whoever believes in Him will receive remission of sins" (Acts 10:43). How does this verse reassure you that forgiveness of sins is available to everyone . . . regardless of the type of sin?

....
....
....
....
....
....
....

9. "For the wages of sin is death, but the gift of God is eternal life in Christ Jesus our Lord" (Romans 6:23). What does Paul mean when he says the wages of sin is death? How are wages different from gifts?

....
....
....
....
....
....
....
....

10. According to this verse, what is required of a person to receive eternal life? What is the one thing that can prevent a person from receiving that gift?

....

....

....

....

....

....

....

TODAY AND TOMORROW

Today: My sins can grieve and quench the Holy Spirit.

Tomorrow: I will ask the Lord to show me areas in my life in which I need to become more like Christ.

CLOSING PRAYER

Lord Jesus, thank You for paying the penalty of our sins on the cross. Thank You for Your incredible gift of forgiveness for our sins. We know that we have failed in the past, and that we will fail again in the future, but we rely on Your promise that when we repent, You will restore us to fellowship with the Father. Help us today not to grieve the Holy Spirit and quench the work He desires to do in us. Help us to continue to become more and more like You.

NOTES AND
PRAYER REQUESTS

Use this space to write any key points, questions, or prayer requests from this week's study.

REPRODUCING CHRIST'S CHARACTER IN US

IN THIS LESSON

Learning: What does the Bible mean when it refers to the "fruit of the Spirit"?

Growing: How can I continually seek to obtain the fruit of the Spirit in my life?

How can you identify a Christian? The Bible's answer is that a Christian will bear the fruit of the Holy Spirit. In other words, a Christian will display the same character qualities that Jesus Christ displayed during His life on this earth. The fruit that we bear is the outward expression that we are true followers of Jesus Christ. This theme of "fruit-bearing" was important in the ministry of Jesus. In the Sermon on the Mount, He said:

Beware of false prophets, who come to you in sheep's clothing, but inwardly they are ravenous wolves. You will know them by their fruits. Do men gather grapes from thornbushes or figs from thistles? Even so, every good tree bears good fruit, but a bad tree bears bad fruit. A good tree cannot bear bad fruit, nor can a bad tree bear good fruit. Every tree that does not bear good fruit is cut down and thrown into the fire. Therefore by their fruits you will know them (Matthew 7:15–20).

Jesus repeated this teaching in more positive terms to His disciples:

I am the true vine, and My Father is the vinedresser. Every branch in Me that does not bear fruit He takes away; and every branch that bears fruit He prunes, that it may bear more fruit. . . . Abide in Me, and I in you. As the branch cannot bear fruit of itself, unless it abides in the vine, neither can you, unless you abide in Me. I am the vine, you are the branches. He who abides in Me, and I in him, bears much fruit; for without Me you can do nothing. If anyone does not abide in Me, he is cast out as a branch and is withered; and they gather them and throw them into the fire, and they are burned. If you abide in Me, and My words abide in you, you will ask what you desire, and it shall be done for you. By this My Father is glorified, that you bear much fruit; so you will be My disciples (John 15:1–2, 4–8).

Without a doubt, Jesus expects us to bear fruit—the fruit of His likeness.

1. "Every branch in Me that does not bear fruit He takes away; and every branch that bears fruit He prunes" (John 15:2). Why does

a gardener prune a branch that already bears fruit? What does this accomplish?

....

....

....

....

....

....

....

2. What does the pruning process involve? What might it involve in a person's life?

....

....

....

....

....

....

....

PETER WAS A FRUIT-BEARER

Peter is a great example of the Holy Spirit working in a person's life to bear fruit. Peter had followed Jesus closely for nearly three years. He had been a witness to His many miracles. He had heard Jesus' sermons. He had watched His life. Peter had even walked on water with the Lord! But in the aftermath of Jesus' arrest in the Garden of Gethsemane, Peter denied three times that he even knew his beloved Master.

However, after Peter received the Holy Spirit on the day of Pentecost, he preached one of the most powerful sermons in the Scriptures.

He proclaimed to the very people whom he had not previously dared to open his mouth:

> Men of Israel, hear these words: Jesus of Nazareth, a Man attested by God to you by miracles, wonders, and signs which God did through Him in your midst, as you yourselves also know—Him, being delivered by the determined purpose and foreknowledge of God, you have taken by lawless hands, have crucified, and put to death (Acts 2:22–23).

Those are not the words of a timid man. Those are words of bold proclamation. Peter was bearing good fruit!

TWO TYPES OF FRUIT

The Bible teaches there are two types of fruit. The first is the fruit of *works and deeds*. Jesus cites this type of fruit in Matthew 7:15–20, where the false prophets are known by their evil words and deeds. The second type of fruit is of *character*. This inner fruit is more important, as what we do is always a natural overflow of who we are. We may be able to hide our bad character behind good deeds for a while, but eventually our true character will display itself.

In his letter to the Galatians, Paul describes the character traits the Lord wants us to have:

> Now the works of the flesh are evident, which are: adultery, fornication, uncleanness, lewdness, idolatry, sorcery, hatred, contentions, jealousies, outbursts of wrath, selfish ambitions, dissensions, heresies, envy, murders, drunkenness, revelries, and the like; of which I tell you beforehand, just as I also told you in time past, that those who practice such things will not inherit the kingdom of God. But the fruit of the Spirit is love, joy, peace, longsuffering, kindness,

goodness, faithfulness, gentleness, self-control. Against such there is no law (Galatians 5:19–23).

God's standard for fruit bearing is righteousness, purity, and obedience to His moral law. Paul repeatedly warned the gentile Christians there is no provision whatsoever in the gospel for impurity. There was no license to sin.

3. What is the difference between the fruit of works and deeds and the fruit of character? Why is character the more important of the two for us to demonstrate?

....
....
....
....
....

4. What does Paul say are the "works of the flesh"? What is the result for those who choose to practice these works?

....
....
....
....
....

5. What does Paul says are the "fruit of the Spirit"? What do you think is the result for those who choose to pursue this type of fruit in their lives?

....
....
....
....

THE NATURE OF FRUIT BEARING

The Bible reveals some important aspects of fruit-bearing in the lives of believers in Christ. *First, followers of Jesus are commanded to bear fruit.* This is not an option. The words that Jesus spoke and the teachings the writers of the New Testament recorded about bearing fruit are commands. *Abide* in Me. *Bear* fruit. *Walk* in the Spirit. *Make* the tree good.

Second, we are to bear good fruit. We have a choice in the type of fruit we will produce. Both Jesus and Paul admonished us to bear fruit that is recognized as good by God. Good fruit is beautiful to behold—it is almost irresistible. Good fruit is also sound—it isn't damaged by disease or bruising. Good fruit bears within it healthy seeds that produce new life. In spiritual terms, good fruit draws others to Christ and is not tainted by sin. Such fruit has within it something that will last forever.

Only the work of the Holy Spirit is truly good, for only His work is eternal and without blemish, compelling others to accept Christ Jesus as their Savior. Fruit that is produced by the Holy Spirit has the same quality of goodness that is found in the Spirit Himself. In Jesus' analogy of the vine, the Holy Spirit is the life force flowing through the vine and producing fruit within us. Jesus was indwelled by the same Holy Spirit who now indwells us, and we produce the same good fruit in our lives that was manifested in Jesus' life.

The Holy Spirit is the source of any goodness in us. We may think that we are good people, but we are not good—apart from the Holy Spirit and the life of Christ that He is producing in us. Our pride causes us to think we can produce goodness on our own.

Third, we are to bear much fruit. Our lives are to be overflowing with the fruit of the Spirit. Our character is to be overflowing with the goodness of Christ Jesus. Our love is to be abundant, our joy is to be exuberant, our peace is to be all-encompassing . . . and so forth. We are to be continually at work in God's kingdom, doing whatever the Lord leads us to do to the best of our ability and with the maximum effort.

Note that the fruit Paul mentions in Galatians 5:22 is *singular*—the "fruit" of the Spirit, not the "fruits" of the Spirit. When we receive the life of the Holy Spirit within us, we get *all* of the Holy Spirit. Thus, all of His traits become our traits. He doesn't award them to us bit by bit. We receive the full nature of the Holy Spirit. However, the abundance of fruit we manifest is subject to the will. We can refuse to do what the Holy Spirit prompts us to do.

6. "I say then: Walk in the Spirit, and you shall not fulfill the lust of the flesh. For the flesh lusts against the Spirit, and the Spirit against the flesh; and these are contrary to one another, so that you do not do the things that you wish" (Galatians 5:16–17). How does the flesh lust against the Spirit? How does the Spirit lust against the flesh?

7. In practical terms, what does it mean to *walk* in the Spirit?

What About the Unfruitful?

Jesus said every branch that doesn't produce is taken away or, as some translations say, "cast away" (see John 15:2). There are two possible interpretations for this phrase "cast away." One is to be lifted up off the ground. In the Middle East, the branches of vines are often left to grow close to the ground rather than trained on wires or trellises, as they are in Europe and the United States. To "cast away" or "take away" a branch can mean to lift it up to train it along a stake or wire. To "cast away" can also mean to cut off and discard. In either case, the vine is moved or removed from its current position.

In the lives of unbelievers, these words should hold a stinging conviction. Those who don't abide in Christ are subject either to being lifted up (which can mean they confess Christ and are saved and made fruitful) or being removed by death. If they don't abide in Christ, they are subject to change—either positive or negative.

Some people try to act as if they are producing fruit. They go through the motions of attending church, doing church work, and claiming to pray and read God's Word. They will do their best to convince you they are people of good character. But they aren't connected to the Vine. They have never been born again and, as a result, they do not receive the lifegiving, fruit-bearing sustenance of the Holy Spirit. They have not been grafted into Christ. Eventually, their state is revealed. The branches wither and are cast away.

If you have any doubt about whether you are grafted into Christ, confess to God that you are a sinner and ask for His forgiveness today. Receive what He freely offers to give you. Then repent of your old ways and rely on the Holy Spirit to produce genuine fruit in your life.

If you are a believer and are not producing much good fruit in your life, the Lord is not going to remove you from Himself. But He is going to continue to convict you of any sin in your life until you let it go, ask for forgiveness, and invite the Lord to cast your sin away from you. The Lord also says that those who are bearing fruit are subject to being pruned so they will bear more fruit. Sin can stop the flow of the Spirit in our lives and result in dead wood in our souls. Neglecting the things of God can cause dead wood. We can become so busy, and have our priorities so out of line, that the flow of the Spirit is thwarted and part of us seems to die out.

If any of these conditions applies to you today, confess this to the Lord, repent of your behavior, receive His forgiveness, and make a new start in your life. Choose actions and attitudes that lead to fruitfulness. Invite the pruning work of the Holy Spirit into your life. Ask Him to show you in which areas you need to change your mind and your behavior.

The reality is that pruning can be painful. It can seem drastic at times. Early in my ministry, I pastored a church in Fruitland, North Carolina. One day, I called on a member of our congregation who was in his apple orchard pruning an apple tree. I was shocked at how severely he was pruning the tree, and I said to him, "You're going to *kill* that tree." He looked at me with the eyes of many years of experience and said, "You stick to preaching, and I'll do the pruning." At times, you may feel as if God is killing you with the severity of His pruning. But be encouraged—He is getting ready for a great harvest of fruit in your life.

8. "My brethren, count it all joy when you fall into various trials, knowing that the testing of your faith produces patience. But let patience have its perfect work, that you may be perfect and complete, lacking nothing" (James 1:2–4). In what ways can "the testing of your faith" produce patience?

9. When you find yourself in the middle of a trial, what is your initial response? What is required on your part to be able to count these trials as "all joy"?

....

....

....

....

....

....

10. "By this we know that we love the children of God, when we love God and keep His commandments. For this is the love of God, that we keep His commandments. And His commandments are not burdensome" (1 John 5:2–3). What commandments might the Holy Spirit be calling you to keep more carefully? What will you do differently this week?

....

....

....

....

....

....

....

Fruit-bearing was never intended to be difficult. A cluster of grapes doesn't have to work at becoming sweet or ripe . . . and neither do we. The fruit-bearing in our lives is automatic if we remain in the Vine. Our job is to abide; His job is to produce fruit in us. As long as we stay true to the Lord, walk in obedience to Him, and allow Him to have control over our lives, the fruit in us grows naturally and according to His time schedule.

We can't force fruit to grow. We can only cling to Jesus and choose to follow the daily leading of the Holy Spirit. *Our heavenly Father* is the Vinedresser. *Jesus* is the Vine. The *Holy Spirit* is the lifegiving force flowing through the Vine. We are the branches that bear His fruit.

TODAY AND TOMORROW

Today: The Holy Spirit brings the full character of God into my life.

Tomorrow: I will prayerfully work on following the Spirit so that my life will be more fruitful.

CLOSING PRAYER

Heavenly Father, thank You that we are growing in maturity. Thank You that the fruit we are bearing is becoming more and more healthy—and there's more of it. We pray that we would continue to experience the presence of the Holy Spirit as we go through our days and listen to His direction in our lives. We pray that the fruit we bear would compel others to realize that the way we lead our lives is different—and that we would draw them to You.

NOTES AND
PRAYER REQUESTS

· ·

Use this space to write any key points, questions, or prayer requests from this week's study.

Relying on the Holy Spirit for Spiritual Gifts

IN THIS LESSON

Learning: What is the difference between spiritual gifts and natural talents?

Growing: What are my spiritual gifts?

Do you feel inadequate in your ability to serve others? Do you often feel incapable of ministry? Do you wish that your ministry to others might be more effective? If so, I have good news for you today! You are not alone. The Holy Spirit will equip you for ministry and then help you do it. The results are completely in His hands, and what the Holy Spirit does is always successful and effective. Paul wrote, "He who calls you is faithful, who also will do it" (1 Thessalonians 5:24).

"But," you may say, "I'm not sure that now is the right time for me to be part of a ministry to others or to take on any service to others." Now is *always* the right time in God's eyes. If you refuse to give yourself to others, you will miss the blessing that comes from giving on earth . . . and you will miss a blessing in heaven. Of equal importance, you will be a hindrance to the work of God. The Lord is counting on you to minister to others, which means He wants for you to serve others, give to others, and help others.

Many people think of *ministry* only in terms of full-time church work or work as a missionary or in a church-related organization. But the truth is that ministry occurs any time we do something in the name of Jesus for the benefit of others. Jesus was clear on this point:

> "I was hungry and you gave Me food; I was thirsty and you gave Me drink; I was a stranger and you took Me in; I was naked and you clothed Me; I was sick and you visited Me; I was in prison and you came to Me."
>
> Then the righteous will answer Him, saying, "Lord, when did we see You hungry and feed You, or thirsty and give You drink? When did we see You a stranger and take You in, or naked and clothe You? Or when did we see You sick, or in prison, and come to You?" And the King will answer and say to them, "Assuredly, I say to you, inasmuch as you did it to one of the least of these My brethren, you did it to Me" (Matthew 25:35–40).

The Lord expects us to be His ministers on earth—to be His hands and feet in the world. He describes those who follow Him as His body. We are to do collectively what Jesus did in His earthly body: minister to others in healing, deliverance, and preaching the good news. And because we are many in number, our ministry multiplies what Jesus did. We are to be like Him in character, in thought, in word, and in deed.

1. When have you given hospitality to strangers or clothed the poor or fed the hungry? When has someone served you in that way?

....

....

....

....

....

2. In what ways are you actually serving Jesus when you do such things for people?

....

....

....

....

....

NATURAL GIFTS VS. SPIRITUAL GIFTS

Our ministry is so important to God the Father that He sent the Holy Spirit to fill us and to enable us to minister. We minister according to the degree we allow the Holy Spirit to work in us. Our ministry is the ministry of the Holy Spirit. We speak the words, but they are His words. We take the actions, but they are His works that He commands us to do. We are the flesh and bones, the personality and talents . . . but He is the motivation and the life.

The Holy Spirit does this by providing us with many gifts that help in our ministry. Another way to think of gifts is as *enablements* or *helps*. Jesus described the Holy Spirit as our Helper. He gives us what we need in the form of spiritual gifts to help us accomplish what He asks us to do.

Spiritual gifts are different from our natural gifts and talents. Natural talents are abilities with which we were born—they are gifts from God given to us in our humanity. They are not divine or spiritual gifts . . . and they never become spiritual gifts. We err if we believe our natural gifts automatically become spiritual gifts when we accept Christ. They do not. Our natural gifts remain after we accept Christ, and they are enhanced or blessed in wonderful ways because of our relationship with Christ Jesus, but they remain as human gifts.

We need to explore, develop, and perfect our natural gifts. After all, God has given them to us to use for His kingdom. We should never downplay our abilities but develop them to their full potential. The Holy Spirit adds His unique gifts to our natural talents and abilities. When we combine what He gives us with what has already been given to us, and when we seek to use both for the Lord's purposes, we are serving God with our whole heart, mind, and soul, and we will be the most effective in our contributions to God's kingdom.

Think of this in terms of doctors who minister to their patients. The doctors do their part, prescribing the best treatment and medicine they know. They perform surgery if is required, or set broken bones or stitch wounds. But only God can heal a sick or injured body. Only God can cause life to overtake disease and cause a sick person to become whole again. The same goes for our work in ministering to others. We do all we can under the direction of the Holy Spirit, but the results of that ministry are His results . . . and His alone. The Holy Spirit causes ministry to take root and become a living testimony in our lives.

The Holy Spirit gives these gifts only to those who follow Christ Jesus—to those who have confessed their sins and received God's forgiveness. Furthermore, in the New Testament, we find that they are broken into three main classifications: (1) motivational gifts, (2) gifts given to the church as a whole, and (3) gifts given for specific situations and circumstances. The Holy Spirit gives these gifts to believers at His discretion . . . but He does give gifts to *every* believer.

3. What natural talents and abilities do you have? How are you using them to serve God?

....

....

....

....

....

4. What natural talents do you see in others around you? How can you encourage them to use those natural abilities for the Lord?

....

....

....

....

....

....

THE MOTIVATIONAL GIFTS

The apostle Paul describes the motivational gifts in Romans 12:6–8, where he writes, "Having then gifts differing according to the grace that is given to us, let us use them: if prophecy, let us prophesy in proportion to our faith; or ministry, let us use it in our ministering; he who teaches, in teaching; he who exhorts, in exhortation; he who gives, with liberality; he who leads, with diligence; he who shows mercy, with cheerfulness." Every believer receives one of these seven motivational gifts. These are listed below with some of the meanings or interpretations of these gifts as they appear in other translations of the Bible:

- *Prophecy*: forth-telling or the speaking out of God's truth
- *Ministry*: serving in practical ways such as hospitality and helping others

- *Teaching*: explaining the Bible so others can understand it and apply it
- *Exhortation*: encouraging others to follow Christ and without hesitation
- *Giving*: contributing to the needs of others
- *Leadership*: having the ability to administer or govern
- *Mercy*: giving aid to sick and needy persons

Paul also describes *how* we are to use these gifts: prophecy, with *faith*; ministry, teaching, and exhortation, with *grace*; giving, with *generosity*; leading, with *diligence*; and mercy, with cheerfulness.

How do you know which of these gifts you have? Examine your life. When a problem arises that you know has a spiritual dimension, what is your first response? Do you immediately want to speak the truth? Do you start to provide help, to give, or to organize others? Do you jump in and act with mercy for people who are hurting? Do you respond with words of encouragement that others stay close to the Lord and obey Him explicitly?

5. Which of these motivational gifts best fits your personality?

....
....
....
....
....
....

6. How can you use this gift in the Lord's service?

....
....
....
....
....

The Gifts Given to the Church

In addition to the endowments the Holy Spirit gives to individual believers, He gives gifts to the church as a whole. These gifts are actually people. As Paul writes: "He Himself gave some to be apostles, some prophets, some evangelists, and some pastors and teachers, for the equipping of the saints for the work of ministry, for the edifying of the body of Christ, till we all come to the unity of the faith and of the knowledge of the Son of God" (Ephesians 4:11–13).

The Holy Spirit gives these gifts to certain people in the church, calling them to be:

- *Apostles:* those who are trailblazers, leaders of new ministry outreaches
- *Prophets:* those who tell God's truth, including the ultimate consequences of following or failing to follow God's will
- *Evangelists:* those who proclaim the gospel of Jesus Christ and inspire others to believe in Him
- *Pastors and teachers:* those who nurture, prepare, and teach believers, equipping them for service to others

Not every person is called to one of these roles within the church, but ministries within a church tend to cluster around these areas of leadership. For example, you may not be called to be a pastor or teacher to a congregation of people, but God may call you to serve as a Sunday school teacher or small-group leader. You are operating in the area of ministry as a teacher to the body of Christ, under the leadership of one who is gifted to lead in that area. Or you may serve on an evangelism team. You are serving in the area of evangelism, under the leadership of one who has been gifted to lead in that area.

You will find great fulfillment serving within the area of ministry to which the Lord calls you. On the other hand, you will find frustration, disappointment, and dissatisfaction in any attempts to serve within an area of ministry to which you are not called by the Holy Spirit.

7. In which area of ministry do you find the Lord leading you with the greatest regularity?

....

....

....

....

....

8. How do you feel when you serve in that capacity? How do you feel when you attempt to serve in other areas?

....

....

....

....

....

UNIQUE GIFTS FOR SPECIFIC CIRCUMSTANCES

The New Testament provides a third set of gifts the Holy Spirit gives to believers. This set of gifts is unique to particular situations and times. In fact, Paul provided this list because he desired to see order restored to the services in the church at Corinth:

> Now concerning spiritual gifts, brethren, I do not want you to be ignorant. . . . There are diversities of gifts, but the same Spirit. There are differences of ministries, but the same Lord.
> And there are diversities of activities, but it is the same God who works all in all. But the manifestation of the Spirit is given to each one for the profit of all: for to one is given the

word of wisdom through the Spirit, to another the word of knowledge through the same Spirit, to another faith by the same Spirit, to another gifts of healings by the same Spirit, to another the working of miracles, to another prophecy, to another discerning of spirits, to another different kinds of tongues, to another the interpretation of tongues. But one and the same Spirit works all these things, distributing to each one individually as He wills. For as the body is one and has many members, but all the members of that one body, being many, are one body, so also is Christ.

For by one Spirit we were all baptized into one body— whether Jews or Greeks, whether slaves or free— and have all been made to drink into one Spirit (1 Corinthians 12:1, 4–13).

Paul's primary concern was not with listing the gifts but in making the point there is only one Holy Spirit. The Corinthians had been idol worshipers prior to their conversion to Christ. They had a different god for each activity, enterprise, and object. Athens, for example, was filled with thousands of idols, each with a specific identity and purpose. Some idol gods were more valued than others. Paul wanted the Corinthians to understand there is only one Holy Spirit—and He manifests Himself in different ways through different individuals as He wills.

As noted, the gifts Paul cited are specific to particular times and events. As the church would gather, different gifts might be manifested depending on the needs of the people and the problems in the church at that time. Paul wanted the believers to understand all of the gifts come from the same Holy Spirit, with no one gift being the definitive manifestation of the Holy Spirit's presence in their midst.

These gifts are bestowed on the believers so one person may be given one gift and another person another gift. All of the gifts are possible, but none of them is assured in any one setting or group of people. In like manner, no one person has his or her identity associated with a particular gift. In other words, one person is not expected to be the prophet at all meetings, and another person the one who gives a word of wisdom. The Holy Spirit speaks and works through this one, and that one, and another one at His direction and for His purposes.

The conclusion we must draw is that a believer may experience one or more of these gifts operating through him during his lifetime, but not necessarily with any predictability or regularity, because the Holy Spirit orchestrates His particular set of gifts to be in operation in each group of people depending on the needs in the group.

The Corinthians apparently had a fondness for the more dramatic gifts, such as healing, tongues, and working miracles. Paul taught them in 1 Corinthians 13 that love is far more important than spiritual gifts. Then, in 1 Corinthians 14, he admonished them to desire prophecy as the foremost gift, so they might speak the truth of God with clarity to nonbelievers and believers alike.

9. Why does Paul reiterate in the above passage that gifts are "by the same Spirit"? What point is he making by repeating this phrase?

....

....

....

....

10. What does Paul's metaphor of the Christian body reveal about the gifts of the Holy Spirit? In what ways can a part of your body serve different functions at different times?

As a believer in Christ, it is important for you to first discern your motivational gift and operate in it, and then follow the leading of the Holy Spirit as He calls you to a particular area of ministry. As you use your motivational gift in ministry, you must continually make yourself available to the Holy Spirit to manifest Himself through you with one or more of the spiritual gifts in 1 Corinthians 12. God knows which natural gifts, talents, abilities, and personality traits He put into your life. He knows which specific spiritual gift is necessary at any given time for the accomplishing of His purposes. He will open the right doors of opportunity for you to minister in a way that is suited to your natural gifts and your motivational gift.

TODAY AND TOMORROW

Today: The Lord gives many gifts to His children,
and they are to be used to serve others.

Tomorrow: I will ask the Lord to show me the gifts He
has given me and how to use them.

CLOSING PRAYER

Heavenly Father, we thank You for loving us. We thank You for the gifts the Holy Spirit gives to each of us who choose to follow You. When we think about how great You are to us—how wonderfully You provide for us—there is nothing that could even come close to the intimate relationship we have with You. Help us today, Lord, to use not only our natural gifts but also our spiritual gifts to be Your hands and feet to a world that is in desperate need of You.

Notes and Prayer Requests

Use this space to write any key points, questions, or prayer requests from this week's study.

PUTTING IT ALL TOGETHER ON SPIRITUAL GIFTS

IN THIS LESSON

Learning: What is the practical outcome of God's promise that I have a spiritual gift?

Growing: What steps can I take to discover and develop my primary motivational gift?

We have learned some critical truths about spiritual gifts throughout this study. For example, we have identified the seven motivational gifts that come from the Holy Spirit, and we have seen how each of us receives one of those gifts when we are indwelt and empowered by God's Spirit. We have learned the difference between our spiritual gifts and our natural talents. And we have come to grips with the fact that using our spiritual gifts for the benefit of God's kingdom is not an option . . . it's a command.

In this lesson, we are going to put everything together in terms of what's next for maximizing our spiritual gifts. If we know we have a gift, and we know we are supposed to use it to minister in God's kingdom, then what steps can we take to get where we are supposed to be? What steps can we take to put it all together and use our gifts as God intended? In particular, we will explore three of those steps: (1) we have a responsibility to discover our gift, (2) we have the opportunity to develop our gift, and (3) we can reflect all of God's gift to us.

WE ARE RESPONSIBLE TO DISCOVER OUR GIFT

I hear it all the time. People tell me, "I want to be more active in ministry, but I haven't figured out yet what my spiritual gift is." Or, "I know the Bible says I have a spiritual gift, but I've been looking, and I still have no idea what it is." For whatever reason, it seems to be a common phenomenon for some people to have a difficult time in discovering their spiritual gift.

But make no mistake: you are responsible to discover your gift. Never forget God's admonition in 1 Peter 4:10: "As each one has received a gift, minister it to one another, as good stewards of the manifold grace of God." The fact that "each one has received a gift" means none of us have any excuse for not discovering what that gift is. More importantly, none of us has any excuse for not using that gift in service to God's kingdom.

Now, having said all that, there are three possible reasons why people may have difficulty discovering their spiritual gift. I want to go through each of those reasons in this lesson so that if you are uncertain about your gift, you can hopefully move forward.

First, you may have trouble identifying your spiritual gift because there are unresolved conflicts in your life. You may have spiritual conflicts— the kinds of issues that cause confusion in your spiritual life and make it difficult to hear from God. Primarily, these conflicts are caused by unresolved sin or strongholds that you have not dealt with properly. If your spiritual life is stagnant and you are not in regular communication or communion with God, it will make it difficult for you to connect with the Spirit as you seek to discover your particular spiritual gift.

Second, you may have trouble discovering your gift if you are not involved in ministry. Now, you may say, "Wait a minute, the reason I'm not serving is because I don't know about my gifting. Once I discover my gift, then I'll serve." But that's backward. Often, your motivational gift will come to the surface as you work to serve God. Your service can reveal your gift, just like studying lots of subjects in school can reveal the one in which you are particularly gifted. You will never have an easy time discovering your gift if you keep it to yourself.

Third, you may be having trouble identifying your spiritual gift if you are attempting to imitate the gift of someone else. I often hear people say, "I really want to have the gift of organization," or, "I wish I had the gift of service." That kind of thinking is counterproductive. Trying to imitate someone else's gift will only confuse things for you. You've been given your specific gift for a reason. Trust the Holy Spirit and learn all you can about your specific gift.

1. "The manifestation of the Spirit is given to each one for the profit of all" (1 Corinthians 12:7). Which of the obstacles mentioned, if any, are impeding your efforts to discover your spiritual gifts and use them to serve others?

2. How did you ultimately come to discover what are your spiritual gifts? How are you actively using those spiritual gifts to advance the kingdom of God?

....

....

....

....

....

3. Where do you have opportunities to help others discover their spiritual gifts?

....

....

....

....

WE CAN DEVELOP OUR GIFT

Every Christian has a spiritual gift—what we have been referring to as a "motivational gift." This is the driving force within that compels you to minister in God's kingdom. Every Christian has at least one of the motivational gifts and, as we just saw, every Christian is responsible for discovering what that gift is in his or her own life.

Once you have discovered your gift, the next step is for you to develop it. The goal is for you to grow in your ability to use that gift so that your influence and impact as a minister in God's kingdom becomes greater and greater. But how do you go about doing this?

Imagine for a moment that you discover early in life that you can sing. You have the talent and the ability to sing well. So, if you want to sing better, what do you do? What next steps do you take? For starters, you would need to study music. You would practice under the instruction of a qualified teacher in order to develop your voice.

You would seek to make connections in the musical world so you could grow as a performer.

This is the same approach that is needed when it comes to developing your spiritual gift. *Namely, you need to actively and intentionally take steps to practice and improve your ability to use your gifts.* The first step I would recommend in this process is for you learn to walk in the Spirit. By this, I mean you examine your life, repent of anything that should not be there—any sin or the effects of sin—and make the choice to submit to God. "Lord, I voluntarily and willingly give You permission to do anything in my life and with my life that You choose. I have accepted by faith Jesus Christ as my Savior and I know my own helplessness. Therefore, I am depending on the Holy Spirit to live His life in and through me, and I give You permission without any reservation to do in me and with me what You choose."

Why is this necessary? Because if you are not walking in the Spirit, you will be walking in the flesh. What this means is that you will be attempting to use your gift and serve God out of your own human energy and your own limited resources. In the end, this will result in you not using your gift profitably. So, if you want to develop your spiritual gift, you need to do so in the context of surrendering your life to the control and guidance of God.

A second step for developing your spiritual gift is to learn the characteristics of that gift. Meaning, what should it look like for that particular gift to be at work in another person's life? What are the qualities that you would identify with someone who was wise and strong in using that gift? And what would that look like in your own life?

For example, say that you have the gift of service, and you want to meet the needs of people as an expression of your faith in God. Well, someone who is skilled and mature at serving others will first and foremost need to be able to identify needs. A person skilled in the gift of service will need to be able to spot an opportunity to serve whenever it comes around. This is a key characteristic of the gift we call service.

You can develop your gift of service by asking God to sharpen your focus when it comes to identifying the needs in your family, in your community, in your church, and in your world. You can ask God to increase your sensitivity to the needs of people. You can also ask God to guide you in your budgeting so that you have resources available when the opportunity arises to meet a need in your church, your community, or your world.

The goal is to identify the specific characteristics of your gift and then work with God to develop and improve those characteristics one by one, step by step. When that happens, your life will begin to weigh more—not your physical body, but your life overall. That is, what you do will carry more influence and more significance with other people. What you say will be more meaningful to them. They will see a widening and a broadening in your spiritual life. They will see more depth to your ministry. Most important, you will grow more motivated in your area of ministry, more fruitful in your work, and more excited to continue on this path of service.

4. "Grow in the grace and knowledge of our Lord and Savior Jesus Christ" (2 Peter 3:18). To what degree are you growing in the use of your spiritual gifts?

   ....
   ....
   ....
   ....

5. What are ways you can *actively* and *intentionally* take steps that will help you practice and improve your ability to use your gifts?

   ....
   ....
   ....
   ....
   ....

6. What would you say are some of the key characteristics of your spiritual gifts?

....

....

....

....

....

....

....

....

WE CAN REFLECT ALL OF GOD'S GIFTS

The third step we can take to effectively use our gifts within God's kingdom is to recognize each Christian has the opportunity to reflect all of the Holy Spirit's motivational gifts. As previously stated, you can reflect all seven of the motivational gifts in your everyday life. Now, you're probably thinking I just contradicted myself. In the previous lesson, I stated that every Christian receives *one* motivational gift. But now I'm saying that Christians can (and should) reflect all *seven* of the spiritual gifts in their lives. How can both be true?

The answer is that while every Christian does receive one primary motivational gift of the Holy Spirit—the gift through which you are most energized and most fruitful as you serve within God's kingdom—it's also true that every Christian is called to imitate Jesus and grow in Christlikeness. Jesus Himself possessed and actively demonstrated all seven spiritual gifts.

Let me run through that again. You have *one* motivational gift as a disciple of Jesus Christ. That will always be true. Yet Jesus is the perfect epitome and the fullest expression of all seven gifts. Therefore, the more you grow in your relationship with Christ, and the more you imitate Him each day, the more you will reflect all seven spiritual gifts as you serve within His kingdom. Now, with that in mind, let's run through seven passages of Scripture that I hope will illustrate this idea even further for you:

- "Pursue love, and desire spiritual gifts, but especially that you may prophesy" (1 Corinthians 14:1).
- "For you, brethren, have been called to liberty; only do not use liberty as an opportunity for the flesh, but through love serve one another" (Galatians 5:13).
- "Let the word of Christ dwell in you richly in all wisdom, teaching and admonishing one another in psalms and hymns and spiritual songs, singing with grace in your hearts to the Lord" (Colossians 3:16).
- "But exhort one another daily, while it is called 'Today,' lest any of you be hardened through the deceitfulness of sin" (Hebrews 3:13).
- "Give, and it will be given to you: good measure, pressed down, shaken together, and running over will be put into your bosom. For with the same measure that you use, it will be measured back to you" (Luke 6:38).
- "Therefore, as the elect of God, holy and beloved, put on tender mercies, kindness, humility, meekness, longsuffering; bearing with one another, and forgiving one another, if anyone has a complaint against another; even as Christ forgave you, so you also must do" (Colossians 3:12–13).

Do you see the thread that is being carried through all seven of those Scripture passages? *Prophesy. Serve. Teach. Exhort. Give. Show mercy.* As a Christian, you are commanded throughout Scripture to practice the seven motivational gifts as you serve in God's kingdom. Even if your primary spiritual gift isn't serving, you are still called to serve. Even if your primary gift isn't giving, you are still called to give. Even if your primary gift isn't teaching, you are still called to teach.

How is it possible to obey these commands? Because of Christ. Jesus lives through you in the power of His Spirit, so you have the capacity to reflect all seven of the motivational gifts when He calls you to do so. You don't *possess* all seven gifts, but you can *reflect* them all because all seven are perfectly contained in Christ.

Maybe as you read through the list of the seven motivational gifts in the previous lesson, you said, "I know this is my motivational gift . . . but there are a couple others that are pretty close. In fact, I've got some qualities of all seven of those gifts." This is exactly right! If you are saved by the grace of God, and if you walk in the Spirit day by day, you will indeed reflect different characteristics of all seven gifts. That is God's goal for you, because you have been called to grow more and more like Christ.

7. Which of the seven passages listed above speaks to you most clearly? Which passage stands out to you the most? Why?

....
....
....
....
....
....
....

8. What theme do you see carried through those verses?

....
....
....
....
....
....
....
....

9. What are some secondary spiritual gifts—not your main gift—
that are regularly evident in your life? How do you know these
secondary gifts are present?

....

....

....

....

....

....

10. What one step will you take this week to continue developing
your spiritual gift as you serve within God's kingdom?

....

....

....

....

....

....

Every believer has a spiritual gift . . . and that includes you.
It is your responsibility to discover your gift. You have the opportunity each day to develop that gift—to exercise it as part of your regular
routine. And as you do so more and more, you will notice that you
not only grow in your specific gift but you also reflect all seven
of God's spiritual gifts within your life and ministry. This is what
should be happening in the life of *every* disciple of Christ.

Unfortunately, what we find in the church is that twenty percent
of the people do eighty percent of the work. In most churches, twenty
percent of the people give eighty percent of the money. In the vast
majority of congregations who gather together week after week, ap-
proximately twenty percent of the people in the church are function-
ing in their gifts, and eighty percent are sitting there as spectators.

Listen again to what Peter said: "As each one has received a gift, minister it to one another, as good stewards of the manifold grace of God" (1 Peter 4:10). May this be true in your life this week.

TODAY AND TOMORROW

Today: God desires that I use my primary motivational gift in service to His kingdom.

Tomorrow: I will take specific steps this week to identify and/or develop my spiritual gifts.

CLOSING PRAYER

Father, we pray that You will make all of us more aware, personally, of Who we have living on the inside of us and the potential we have to be a force for good in the lives of others. Teach us, Lord, to take the next steps—whatever those may be—in using the gifts You have provided to us for the work of Your kingdom. Help us to discover our gifts, embrace the opportunities You provide to develop our gifts, and allow our gifts to be a reflection of Christ to the world. We pray this, Lord, in the name of Jesus, knowing that it is Your will. Amen.

NOTES AND
PRAYER REQUESTS

Use this space to write any key points, questions, or prayer requests from this week's study.

MAKING OUR MINISTRIES EFFECTIVE

Learning: What is the purpose of spiritual gifts?

Growing: How should I be serving the Body of Christ?

So far in this study, we have discussed the unique blend of spiritual gifts the Holy Spirit bestows on believers in Christ Jesus. In this lesson, we are going to focus on the reasons why the Holy Spirit gives believers those gifts. As we examine the evidence in Scripture, I believe we find that there are four main reasons for the bestowal of such spiritual gifts in our lives: (1) they are for the common good of all believers, (2) they equip us for further ministry, (3) they are for our encouragement, and (4) they are for our edification.

Ultimately, all of the gifts are intended to be manifested so Jesus Christ is lifted up and God the Father is glorified. Whenever the spiritual gifts call attention to our own lives as the ones who are manifesting them, we are in error. All spiritual gifts belong to God and come from Him. All praise should thus be directed to God for the results or benefits of those gifts.

Furthermore, we are to hold these gifts and use them as good stewards of God's grace. We are to recognize at all times that we didn't create these gifts or authorize their use, and we have no right to claim them in a prideful manner. We are to use them wisely for the purpose that their true owner, the Holy Spirit, intended. The servant may use the master's utensils, china, and silverware to prepare and serve a magnificent meal for the benefit of the master's guests, but the servant does not own the utensils, china, and silverware. In like manner, we employ the gifts of the Spirit for the benefit of others.

Of course, this does not mean we are to take the bestowal of spiritual gifts lightly. We are to cherish them, hold them in high regard, and manifest them in our lives with boldness, confidence, and dignity. As Peter wrote, "If anyone speaks, let him speak as the oracles of God. If anyone ministers, let him do it as with the ability which God supplies, that in all things God may be glorified through Jesus Christ, to whom belong the glory and the dominion forever and ever" (1 Peter 4:11).

The gifts we receive from the Holy Spirit are for us to use for the benefit of others. Jesus said, "Freely you have received, freely give" (Matthew 10:8). Freely we have received of the Holy Spirit . . . and so freely we give back to others. What we receive from God we are expected to share with others for their benefit more than for our benefit. We, in turn, receive from others the benefit from the gifts the Holy Spirit gives to them. In this way, we are formed into a body of believers and are built up as a community of faith.

1. What does it mean to minister "as with the ability which God supplies"? How else might a person minister to others?

....

....

....

....

....

2. How might spiritual gifts be misused to serve oneself instead of others? How might the praise and honor be misdirected in such situations?

....

....

....

....

....

FOR THE COMMON GOOD
AND EQUIPPING THE SAINTS

As we have discussed, the gifts of the Holy Spirit are to be used "for the profit of all" (1 Corinthians 12:7). When one person hurts in the body of Christ, all are hurt. When one is blessed, all are blessed. The gifts are intended to bring healing, wholeness, and benefit to a *body* of believers. The gifts of the Holy Spirit are for the benefit of all God's children.

The motivational gift you receive from the Holy Spirit is given *to* you, but it is *for* others. If you are given a role in the church, your gift is for service to others. If you are given a spiritual gift—whether it is "the word of wisdom through the Spirit . . . the word of knowledge . . . faith . . . gifts of healings . . . the working of miracles . . . prophecy . . . discerning of spirits . . . different kinds of tongues . . . the interpretation of tongues" (1 Corinthians 12:7–10)—you are to manifest it and help others. Always ask, "How can I use this gift for the common good?"

In the same way, you should use your gift to equip the saints. Recall that in Ephesians 4:11–12, Paul tells us the gifts to the church— the placing of apostles, prophets, evangelists, pastors, and teachers within the church—are for this purpose: "equipping of the saints for the work of ministry." The purpose of a good sermon is to inspire the congregation to be obedient and faithful in their walk with the Lord. The purpose of a good Bible lesson is to help people grow in faith and in their understanding about how to apply God's Word to their lives.

Paul also wrote, "We are [God's] workmanship, created in Christ Jesus for good works, which God prepared beforehand that we should walk in them" (Ephesians 2:10). You are God's masterpiece. He has saved you, gifted you with natural abilities and talents, protected and provided for you, and now, through the Holy Spirit, He has given you spiritual gifts. At the same time, He has prepared a place for you to use those gifts.

Furthermore, even as the Lord was preparing you to serve in His church, He was preparing others to receive what you have to give. He has paved the way for your ministry to be effective. In other words, others need what the Holy Spirit prompts you to prepare and give to them. You, in turn, need what others have been prompted by the Holy Spirit to give to you.

When you recognize that every person who crosses your path has been allowed to cross your path by the Holy Spirit, for a purpose that has benefit to you, what a marvelous adventure you experience in daily living! Furthermore, if a believer crosses your path, you can know that believer has been put there by the Holy Spirit for the express purpose of equipping you in some way for the work of ministry. There is something you are to learn or acquire from every conversation, and every encounter, with another saint of God.

3. What does it mean that the gifts of the Spirit are for the "equipping of the saints for the work of ministry"?

4. When has the Lord brought you together with another Christian so you could give your gift to him or her? When have you been on the receiving end of this blessing?

....

....

....

....

....

FOR ENCOURAGEMENT
OF THE BELIEVERS

We all need encouragement in our daily lives. We all need someone to build us up and help us see our value and worth before the Lord. The devil and the world's systems will grind you down and wear you out. You need others in the body of Christ to remind you that you are God's unique and irreplaceable creation called to unique and irreplaceable places of ministry. You need to be reminded of God's love for you and of your importance to the church.

Paul addressed this need for encouragement in his letter to the Corinthians:

If the foot should say, "Because I am not a hand, I am not of the body," is it therefore not of the body? And if the ear should say, "Because I am not an eye, I am not of the body," is it therefore not of the body? If the whole body were an eye, where would be the hearing? If the whole were hearing, where would be the smelling? But now God has set the members, each one of them, in the body just as He pleased. And if they were all one member, where would the body be?

But now indeed there are many members, yet one body. And the eye cannot say to the hand, "I have no need of you"; nor again the head to the feet, "I have no need of you." No, much rather, those members of the body which seem to be weaker are necessary. And those members of the body which we think to be less honorable, on these we bestow greater honor; and our unpresentable parts have greater modesty, but our presentable parts have no need. But God composed the body, having given greater honor to that part which lacks it, that there should be no schism in the body, but that the members should have the same care for one another. And if one member suffers, all the members suffer with it; or if one member is honored, all the members rejoice with it (1 Corinthians 12:15–26).

As the gifts of the Spirit are shared among believers, under the direction and orchestration of the Spirit, you can't help but have an awareness that God counts each of His children as highly valuable in His church. No matter your social status, profession, or lot in life, you can be used by the Holy Spirit in valuable roles of ministry.

Now, you may say, "I don't see how God can use me. I'm totally inadequate." Or you may say, "I can't be used by God. I will just fail." But God says, "Let Me use you. I'll use whatever you do and be in whatever you do, and that means it will be a blessing to someone. I never fail, and since I'm in whatever good you do for My body, whatever you do won't fail."

Your spiritual gifts should always bring encouragement to others. Even if you have a motivational gift of exhortation, the ultimate purpose of exhortation is to say to another person, "You can follow Christ. You can walk in obedience and righteousness before Him. You can remain faithful to the Lord regardless of what situations you face."

If you operate in the gift of evangelism, it is important to exercise your gift so people hear the good news that Jesus came to save them from their sins—and not focus solely on the existence of hell and eternal damnation for the unsaved. If you give a word of wisdom to others, that word of wisdom is to give them direction that will point them toward God and toward His answers in life. Such a word will automatically point such individuals away from danger and sin . . . but it should do so as an encouraging word to receive God's best in their lives.

5. "But God composed the body, having given greater honor to that part which lacks it, that there should be no schism in the body" (1 Corinthians 12:24–25). Which part of your body would you not miss if it were removed? What does this suggest about the need for all believers and all gifts in the church?

....
....
....
....
....
....
....

6. God has set each believer to perform a specific function in the body, "just as He pleased." What does this suggest about the value of your gifts?

....
....
....
....
....
....
....

FOR EDIFICATION

Spiritual gifts are to be exercised for the edification of the church. *Edification* means the "building up" or the "strengthening" of the church. The apostle Paul wrote, "Since you are zealous for spiritual gifts, let it be for the edification of the church that you seek to excel" (1 Corinthians 14:12). All things are to be done so the church body as a whole might be perfected—so sin might be cleansed from a group of believers, so healing and wholeness might occur individually and collectively, so conflicts might be resolved and relationships reconciled, and so losses might be restored and excesses trimmed away.

In writing about the gifts to the church, Paul gave an outline of what edification produces: "We all come to the unity of the faith and of the knowledge of the Son of God, to a perfect man, to the measure of the stature of the fullness of Christ; that we should no longer be children, tossed to and fro and carried about with every wind of doctrine, by the trickery of men, in the cunning craftiness of deceitful plotting, but, speaking the truth in love, may grow up in all things into Him who is the head—Christ" (Ephesians 4:13–15.)

A thoroughly edified group of believers would thus have the following profile:

- Unity of the faith and of the knowledge of the Son of God
- Manifesting the fullness of Christ
- No longer confused by the latest doctrinal trends
- No longer deceived by the trickery of men
- No longer engaged in plotting or cunning craftiness
- Speaking the truth in love

Paul concluded the end result of edification is a "whole body"—one that is "joined and knit together by what every joint supplies, according to the effective working by which every part does its share" (Ephesians 4:16). As with the manifestation of spiritual gifts, this process is to be marked by love. So, as you think over your motivational gifts and your role of ministry, ask yourself, "Am I manifesting the gifts of the Spirit so that the entire body of Christ is built up? Are my gifts contributing toward our perfection as a group of believers in Christ Jesus?"

7. In what ways do spiritual gifts "join and knit together" the body of Christ? Give specific examples.

....

....

....

....

....

....

....

8. What part do you play in your local body of Christians? Are you performing that function fully and willingly? Explain.

....

....

....

....

....

....

....

....

LASTING BENEFITS

The gifts of the Holy Spirit bless you now, and they bless you forever, when they are manifested in ministry that is for the common good, that equips the saints for further ministry, that is marked by encouragement, and that results in edification. Paul declared to the Corinthians, "We are God's fellow workers; you are God's field, you are God's building" (1 Corinthians 3:9). He then followed that statement with these sobering words:

According to the grace of God which was given to me, as a wise master builder I have laid the foundation, and another builds on it. But let each one take heed how he builds on it. For no other foundation can anyone lay than that which is laid, which is Jesus Christ. Now if anyone builds on this foundation with gold, silver, precious stones, wood, hay, straw, each one's work will become clear; for the Day will declare it, because it will be revealed by fire; and the fire will test each one's work, of what sort it is. If anyone's work which he has built on it endures, he will receive a reward. If anyone's work is burned, he will suffer loss; but he himself will be saved, yet so as through fire (1 Corinthians 3:10–15).

Your use of the Holy Spirit's gifts in ministry is not just for here and now. They should have an eternal ring to them, and they will if they are truly gifts from the Holy Spirit. When you invite the Holy Spirit to work through you to bless others, He will do so. He is eternal, and whatever He does through you will have an eternal quality to it. If you want to minister in effective ways, you must want your ministry to last for all eternity. This can happen only as you allow the Holy Spirit to help you in any act of ministry that you undertake. It can happen only as you regard each spiritual gift as coming from Him and being used for the perfecting of His body.

9. What sort of ministry will endure the test of fire? What sort of ministry will be burned up?

....

....

....

....

....

....

....

10. Will your own ministry stand the test of fire? How can you increase the eternal value of what you do for the Lord today?

....

....

....

....

....

....

TODAY AND TOMORROW

Today: The Holy Spirit's gifts are for the benefit of others, and the results are eternal.

Tomorrow: I will ask the Lord to teach me how to produce fruit that will last forever.

CLOSING PRAYER

Holy Spirit, we praise You for making things so simple for us. We like to make things complex, but You have made it so we are able to live by faith, moment by moment, trusting in Your indwelling presence to accomplish what we could never accomplish on our own. Help us to use the gifts You provide for the good of all believers. Help us to use Your gifts as we pursue opportunities for ministry. Help us to use Your gifts to encourage others. And help us to use the gifts You provide not for our own glory but to bring glory to God and point others toward His grace. Amen.

NOTES AND
PRAYER REQUESTS

Use this space to write any key points, questions, or prayer requests from this week's study.

How to Acquire Spiritual Discernment

IN THIS LESSON

Learning: What is spiritual discernment and why should I want it?

Growing: What steps can I take to receive a greater level of spiritual discernment in my life?

If you've been around the block a few times, as I have, then you probably know there's a difference between intelligence and discernment. A big difference. *Intelligence* is a person's raw brainpower. It's the ability to process information, memorize data, and think efficiently. *Discernment* is the ability to make judgments. It's the ability to evaluate different options and make choices that are wise—choices that are beneficial rather than harmful.

This is why it's possible for a person to be extremely intelligent yet still make terrible decisions in their lives—because they lack discernment. The same idea applies when it comes to spiritual intelligence and spiritual discernment, which is the topic for this lesson. I've met a lot of people who are spiritually intelligent. They have degrees. They know doctrine. They can cite you chapter and verse all through the Bible. Yet, in many cases, they don't make the kinds of decisions we would expect Jesus to make. Why? Because they lack spiritual discernment.

By this, I mean that spiritual discernment is the ability to be guided by the Holy Spirit to see things from God's point of view. It is to allow the Holy Spirit to help you understand the world in a similar way to how God understands it. As a result, those who are spiritually discerning see things from a different perspective than what we might call a "rational" mind. The spiritual discernment the Holy Spirit provides gives you the ability to distinguish between right and wrong, what is good and what is best, what is wise and unwise, what is truth and error, and what is the self-will and the will of God.

Every single one of us needs spiritual discernment. Every single one of us needs to be able to see beneath the surface and perceive things not merely how they *seem* to be but how they *truly* are. In this lesson, we will explore how we can get this kind of spiritual discernment. Specifically, we will see that we can gain spiritual discernment by (1) seeking for it, (2) submitting to the Holy Spirit, (3) studying God's Word, and (4) following God's instructions.

1. Who serves as an example of spiritual discernment in your life? What characteristics or attributes does that person possess?

....
....
....
....
....

2. What are some of the dangers in not having spiritual discernment? What consequences have you seen in your life or the lives of others for not having spiritual discernment?

....

....

....

....

....

....

SEEK SPIRITUAL DISCERNMENT

There are many things we can only find when we look for them, and spiritual discernment is a great example. By that I mean it's not automatic. Becoming a Christian doesn't mean that all of a sudden you can look at the Bible, understand it, and therefore you have spiritual discernment. That's not how it works, and we know that because there are many Christians who go through life making terrible, painful, disastrous decisions due to a lack of spiritual discernment.

You see, one of the main reasons believers don't have spiritual discernment is that they don't even know it's available. They go through life believing they have everything they need inside themselves to be spiritually mature, which of course is way off the mark. As long as we're prideful enough to think we can handle everything life throws our way—"I've got the education I need"; "I've got the experience"; "I've got the intelligence"—as long as that's true, we will never seek spiritual discernment. Which means we will never find it.

King David highlighted the value of seeking spiritual discernment when he wrote, "Teach me good judgment and knowledge, For I believe Your commandments. Before I was afflicted I went astray, But now I keep Your word" (Psalm 119:66–67).

David had been "afflicted," meaning he had experienced suffering and hardship in the world. As a result, he learned that he didn't know everything. He learned that he needed help. And so he turned to the Lord to seek discernment—"good judgment and knowledge."

Most people look at life through their physical eyes and never see what they miss. They listen through their physical ears and never hear what they should have been attuned to. They are sensitive to many things, but not to the Spirit of God. Therefore, they miss some of the greatest experiences in life—some of the greatest times of worship, some of the most wonderful opportunities to be obedient, and some of the greatest privileges that God offers to us. All because they do not seek spiritual discernment. Don't let that be true of you.

3. Solomon prayed, "Give to Your servant an understanding heart to judge Your people, that I may discern between good and evil. For who is able to judge this great people of Yours?" (1 Kings 3:9). How does this show he was seeking spiritual discernment?

....

....

....

....

4. What does it look like for you to seek spiritual discernment?

....

....

....

....

SUBMIT TO THE HOLY SPIRIT

In his first letter to the Corinthians, Paul gave us the following clear understanding of how the Holy Spirit works to produce spiritual discernment in our lives:

But God has revealed them to us through His Spirit. For the Spirit searches all things, yes, the deep things of God. For what man knows the things of a man except the spirit of the man which is in him? Even so no one knows the things of God except the Spirit of God. Now we have received, not the spirit of the world, but the Spirit who is from God, that we might know the things that have been freely given to us by God (1 Corinthians 2:10–12).

Each and every believer in Christ is indwelt by the Holy Spirit. He joins with us at the moment of salvation. He seals us as a child of God forever. But that's not the end of His work in our lives . . . it's just the beginning. The Spirit has multiple ways of ministering in and through us each day.

As Paul noted, one example of the Holy Spirit's work is that He helps us discern between God's truth and the world's truth. If we are to have any hope of spiritual discernment, we must have the Spirit of God revealing what is truth from God's viewpoint. As Paul said, "no one knows the things of God except the Spirit of God."

Paul added, "But the natural man does not receive the things of the Spirit of God, for they are foolishness to him; nor can he know them, because they are spiritually discerned" (2 Corinthians 2:14). This is an incredible principle, because it shows us how we are in absolute dependence on God's Spirit to interpret spiritual truth for us. There are many truths and doctrines in God's Word that seem silly to the world around us—they seem like "foolishness." Yet they are vital elements of our faith when we understand them through the lens of God's redemptive work throughout history and His plan for the future.

Think about it: how would you and I ever understand God's redemptive plan apart from the enlightening power of the Holy Spirit? We wouldn't. We couldn't. How would we understand what justification is all about? Justification says we are no longer declared guilty by God. Well, that doesn't make sense—each of us knows we are guilty when it comes to sin, so how can we be declared not guilty? The Spirit of God gives us discernment to understand that, as disciples of Jesus, we've been pardoned from our sin through His sacrifice on the cross.

Just as important, the Holy Spirit gives us discernment to see and understand that we don't go to heaven because of our good works. We see this misunderstanding all the time in our culture. People say, "I believe God is good. He's a God of love. Therefore, if I'm good— if I do more good things than bad things—I feel certain I'm going to heaven." This makes sense based this world's view of things, but it is utter foolishness from God's viewpoint.

The only way we can tell the difference between the two is by submitting to the work of the Holy Spirit in our lives and allowing Him to produce spiritual discernment within us.

5. How would you describe "the spirit of the world"? What are some of its values?

....

....

....

....

....

....

....

6. What are some other biblical doctrines or values that you know that would seem like "foolishness" to most of the world?

....

....

....

....

....

....

....

Study God's Word

Here's a simple truth. If you want to have spiritual discernment, you must be willing to study the Word of God. If you want to know what God thinks about something—and especially if you want to train your thinking to match His own—you need to go to His guidebook. This is because the Bible is God's revelation of Himself.

God could have certainly given us just a couple sheets of paper that efficiently and succinctly laid out who He is and what He wants from us as His people. He could have inspired one of the biblical authors to simply say on His behalf, "Here's who I am, here's who Jesus is, here's who the Holy Spirit is. And on the next two pages, you will find out how the Father, Son, and Holy Spirit operate and how we think." But as human beings with limited understanding and attention spans, what would we do with those kinds of instructions? We would skim through the list . . . and then we would forget it. That kind of communication would not make the lasting impact we need.

Therefore, God has wisely unfolded the truth of Himself not through a list but through a series of stories—all woven together into a miraculous unity from Genesis 1 to Revelation 22. As we read and study this story, this Book, the Spirit of God opens our minds and our hearts to *see* who God is, what He is like, and what He expects from His people. We see God illustrated in the pages of His Word. How did God operate in the Garden of Eden? How did He operate with Abraham? How did He work in David's life? In Daniel's life? How did He reveal Himself to Paul? How did He make Himself known to Peter? How does God respond to wickedness and ungodliness among the nations? How does He communicate to the church?

The narratives in the Bible help us to discover who God is. As the author of Hebrews writes, "For the word of God is living and powerful, and sharper than any two-edged sword, piercing even to the division of soul and spirit, and of joints and marrow, and is a discerner of the thoughts and intents of the heart" (Hebrews 4:12). The Bible is not a dead book; it's alive. And it's a book about *life*. It's not a dry list of information.

If we are going to have spiritual discernment, we have to know the mind of God. Where do we find out about the mind of God? We go to the Book and see how He operates there—what He reveals about Himself. As we do, we will find that He is never inconsistent. He is always the same. This book is not only current, it's not only applicable, but it also never changes. It is the ageless revelation of the Living God who is dependably the same . . . forever.

For these reasons and more, the Word of God is the basis of all spiritual discernment. So study it. Know it. Live it and breathe it, so it can live and breathe through you.

7. "All Scripture is given by inspiration of God, and is profitable for doctrine, for reproof, for correction, for instruction in righteousness" (2 Timothy 3:16). When have you seen the truth of this statement in your own life?

   ....

   ....

   ....

   ....

   ....

   ....

8. What is one way God has changed your thinking by your engagement with the Bible?

   ....

   ....

   ....

   ....

   ....

   ....

Follow God's Instructions

If you want to grow in spiritual discernment, you have to seek for it, depend on the Holy Spirit to work in and through your life, and study the Word of God. But finally, if you want to have spiritual discernment, you must also follow God's instructions.

What do I mean by this? Well, there is an interesting moment in the book of Ezekiel where God was giving orders about the role of the priests in Israel. One of those orders reads, "And they shall teach My people the difference between the holy and the unholy, and cause them to discern between the unclean and the clean" (Ezekiel 44:23). Part of the priests' responsibility as God's servants was to teach the people *discernment*. God had given His people laws throughout the Old Testament, and the priests had the job of helping the people understand those laws.

The priests provided guidance, for instance, on matters such as what things the people could eat and should not eat, what was considered "clean" and what was considered "unclean," what they could touch and were not supposed to touch, what places the people could go and were not allowed to go, and the like. This lines up with what we read from King David in Psalm 119:66: "Teach me good judgment and knowledge, for I believe Your commandments." There was an element of instruction involved.

Here's my point: the fact that you and I can be instructed in discernment means the process of gaining discernment is progressive, not static. It means we gain discernment bit by bit throughout our lives. It's something we can learn . . . but it requires us to be active in seeking it, in studying God's Word, and then in *obeying* the instructions we are given.

Let's say that you bought a fancy piece of machinery from a salesperson—something complicated to operate. And let's say that salesperson took the time to write out specific, detailed instructions on how you could operate that machinery in order to maximize its effect in your life or in your business. Wouldn't that be a valuable set of instructions?

But what if you took those instructions home and then stashed them away in a drawer for a week? Then two weeks? Then six months? That would be a waste! There is no point in receiving instructions if you have no intention to follow them—if you have no intention to do what they say. In a similar way, there's no point to seeking spiritual discernment by submitting to the Holy Spirit, actively searching out God's Word, and then failing to follow through on what you learn during each of those processes. There is no point to growing in spiritual discernment if you never intend to put it into practice.

If you want spiritual discernment, you must be willing to follow the instructions you receive. Otherwise, any discernment that does take root in your life will simply wither and die.

9. "Be doers of the word, and not hearers only, deceiving yourselves" (James 1:22). What does it mean to be a "doer" of the word? Why is this important?

....

....

....

....

10. What are some obstacles that hinder you from following the instructions you receive from God? What can you do this week to knock down those obstacles in your life?

....

....

....

....

....

Please hear me when I say this: don't wait for spiritual discernment. Yes, it's true the Holy Spirit is our Source for spiritual discernment, but it also takes discipline on our part. It takes time. It takes intention and effort. That being the case, let me say spiritual discernment is worth the effort. It's worth every resource you invest through God's Spirit. Spiritual discernment will impact every single decision you make. Who you marry or do not marry. What business you go into—or avoid. How you raise your children. When you have spiritual discernment, you can analyze every aspect of your life from God's viewpoint and through what the Word of God says.

TODAY AND TOMORROW

Today: The Holy Spirit is fully ready and able to produce spiritual discernment in my mind and heart.

Tomorrow: I am ready to be active, not passive, in seeking spiritual discernment and following God's instructions.

CLOSING PRAYER

Father, we pray You will help those who are struggling in knowing what is the right decision to make. Grant them the wisdom to rely on the Holy Spirit's guidance to help them distinguish between the value of that which is eternal and the value of that which is temporal and passing. And in our own lives, Lord, we pray that You would increase our spiritual discernment. Let us continue to seek for it, submit to Your Holy Spirit for it, study Your Word, and follow Your instructions. Thank You, Lord, for giving us Your Word. Let it be a guide to us today.

NOTES AND
PRAYER REQUESTS

Use this space to write any key points, questions, or prayer requests from this week's study.

RELYING ON THE HOLY SPIRIT FOR DAILY GUIDANCE

─── **IN THIS LESSON** ───

Learning: What is the day-to-day role of the Holy Spirit in my life?

Growing: How can I understand God's will for me?

To whom do you turn for daily guidance in how to live your life? The Bible states the only Guide worth having in your life is the Holy Spirit. He is the only One who knows your past completely from the moment you were conceived to this present day. He is the only One who knows your future completely—from this day extending into eternity. He is the One who knows God's plan and purpose for you today and each day of your life on this earth.

When you turn to people for advice, you must be aware that in many cases they will tell you only what they think you want to hear.

They want to make you feel good so you will like them more, which in turn makes them feel good. If you seek advice from another person, get advice that is honest, true to God's Word, and without ulterior motives. Even as you receive advice from others, you must check it against the Holy Spirit's witness in your spirit and against the Bible to verify that the advice is right for you in your given circumstance.

Only the Holy Spirit knows what is fully good and right for you on a daily basis. Any other opinion can be only a part of the full truth that is known by the Holy Spirit. Jesus repeatedly referred to the Holy Spirit as the Spirit of truth. The Spirit of truth is like an inner compass—always pointing you toward what Jesus would be, say, or do in any situation.

1. "He will glorify Me, for He will take of what is Mine and declare it to you" (John 16:14). What does it mean that the Holy Spirit "will take of what is Mine and declare it to you"? How does this glorify Christ?

   ....

   ....

   ....

   ....

   ....

   ....

2. In what ways has the Holy Spirit served as the "Spirit of truth" in your life?

   ....

   ....

   ....

   ....

   ....

   ....

GOD HAS ALWAYS SOUGHT TO GUIDE HIS PEOPLE

Even before Jesus came into this earth, the Holy Spirit was guiding God's people. In fact, it has been God's desire for His people throughout the ages. Numerous verses in the Old Testament point toward God's guidance. Certainly, He provided daily instruction for His people as they left Egypt and crossed the wilderness to the land God had promised to them.

God's guidance was then manifested as a pillar of cloud by day and a pillar of fire by night. (In the Bible, the symbol of fire is usually associated with the Holy Spirit.) The leaders of the early church relied on the Holy Spirit to give them this kind of personal guidance, and we are wise to do likewise. In Romans 8:14 and Galatians 5:18, Paul refers to our being "led by the Spirit." This is to be the norm of the Christian life.

The Bible describes at least three wonderful results of the Holy Spirit's guidance in our lives.

First, the Holy Spirit convicts of sin, of righteousness, and of judgment. The Holy Spirit gives us a clear understanding of what is wrong, what is right, and how to tell the difference.

Second, the Holy Spirit reveals the truth of any situation to us to keep us from stumbling or from entering into error. He truly "delivers us from evil" in this way (Matthew 6:13). He will help us "walk circumspectly, not as fools but as wise, redeeming the time, because the days are evil" (Ephesians 5:15–16). He will lead us to right choices, right relationships, and right priorities. He will help us to make the most of our time each day.

Third, the Holy Spirit searches our hearts. He reveals to us our deepest motives and our deepest desires. In so doing, He shows us who we really are and how we can become more like Jesus. The Holy Spirit gives us guidance to help us mature in the Lord and become more like Christ day by day.

3. "Trust in the LORD with all your heart, And lean not on your own understanding; In all your ways acknowledge Him, And He shall direct your paths" (Proverbs 3:5–6). What does it mean to "lean on your own understanding"? How is this different from trusting the Lord? Give practical examples of each.

....

....

....

....

....

....

....

4. "The LORD is my shepherd; I shall not want. He makes me to lie down in green pastures; He leads me beside the still waters" (Psalm 23:1–2). Consider the shepherd and sheep imagery in these verses. What do they teach about the Holy Spirit's work in a believer's life?

....

....

....

....

....

....

....

CONDITIONS FOR THE HOLY SPIRIT'S GUIDANCE

Now, there are some conditions placed upon the guidance of the Holy Spirit in our lives. *First, we must believe in Jesus.* In order to receive the guidance of the Holy Spirit throughout our days, we must first accept Christ as our personal Savior, confess our sins, and receive God's forgiveness. The Holy Spirit does not give daily guidance to nonbelievers—the only direction the Holy Spirit gives to them is the conviction they need to accept Christ.

Second, we must stay yielded to the Holy Spirit. We must say yes to the Holy Spirit when He prompts us to take a certain action or say a certain word to others. We must give mental assent to the Holy Spirit's direction . . . and we must actually *obey* His prompting and follow through in doing or saying what He has called us to do or say. We can know that we are yielded to Him when we are able to say to Him, "Here is what I desire, but if Your answer is *no* to this, it is all right. I will choose to do what You say."

Third, we must believe we will receive His guidance. We must expect the Holy Spirit to speak in the inner person and direct us toward good and away from evil. We must be intentional and focused in this. We are much more likely to hear what the Holy Spirit has to say to us if we are actively listening for Him to speak. We are much more likely to see the Holy Spirit's direction if we are looking for His signs. The author of Hebrews tells us, "But without faith it is impossible to please Him, for he who comes to God must believe that He is, and that He is a rewarder of those who diligently seek Him" (Hebrews 11:6). We are to be diligent in seeking His guidance, asking for it, watching for it, anticipating it, and receiving it.

Fourth, we are to wait upon the Lord until we receive His guidance. In Psalm 27:14, King David tells us, "Wait on the Lord; be of good courage, and He shall strengthen your heart; Wait, I say, on the Lord!" Until the Lord tells us what role we are to play, we are not to act. If we don't know what to say, we remain silent and pray. If we don't know where to turn, we stay on our knees until His direction is clear. Although our desire will be to rush ahead, we can't become impatient in our desire to hear from the Lord—we must wait and listen. His guidance will come.

5. "But those who wait on the Lord shall renew their strength; they shall mount up with wings like eagles, they shall run and not be weary, they shall walk and not faint" (Isaiah 40:31). What does it mean to wait on the Lord? Give practical examples.

....
....
....
....
....
....
....

6. What is the promise in this verse for those who wait on the Lord? When have you rushed ahead of the Lord's guidance? What happened as a result?

....
....
....
....
....
....

HOW GUIDANCE IS IMPARTED TO US

The Holy Spirit imparts His daily guidance to in several ways. *First, He speaks to us through the words of the Bible.* The Spirit will never lead us to do anything that is contrary to God's Word. If we believe that we have heard the Lord speak in our heart, we need to go to the Word of God to confirm that message. Often as we are reading God's Word, He will speak in our hearts, "Do this. This is for you. That's My desire for you." He brings certain passages to life for us.

We can always find a phrase or verse in the Bible to back up what we desire to do in our human nature. Now, in saying this, I am not at all suggesting that we go to the Bible to "get a verse" as justification for the decision that we have already chosen to make. That is not what it means to be led by the Spirit. Rather, I am recommending that we read our Bible daily with this prayer on our lips: "Holy Spirit, speak to me through the Word. Just as You inspired men of old to write these words, inspire me about how to apply these words to my life."

The Holy Spirit gives us the *principles* of the Word of God to guide us in making decisions. In many cases, there won't be a specific story or passage of Scripture that will seem to speak directly to our situation. But the principles of God's Word are true and eternal. They can be applied to give us guidance in making choices and decisions. Given this, whenever we are making a decision, we need to ask, "Will God be glorified in this? Can I give thanks to God for this? Can I do this in the name of Jesus, fully expecting His blessing, His provision, and His stamp of approval?" If we can answer yes to these questions about a decision, we can be assured that we are making the decision within the principles of God's Word.

Second, the Holy Spirit speaks to us through circumstances. As we wait upon the Lord and trust Him for guidance, the Holy Spirit often opens certain doors in our lives and closes certain other ones. As Paul wrote, "All things work together for good to those who love God, to those who are the called according to His purpose" (Romans 8:28). We should remember that all the circumstances of our lives are under God's direct sovereignty, and He allows things to happen for His own purposes.

Third, the Holy Spirit speaks to us in the stillness of our hearts with a word of conviction or assurance. When the Holy Spirit is directing us away from something harmful, we often will have a heaviness or a feeling of trouble, foreboding, or uneasiness in our spirits. When the Holy Spirit is directing us toward things that are helpful to us, we will tend to feel a deep inner peace, an eagerness to see what God will do, and a feeling of joy.

The Holy Spirit often works predominantly through one of these methods to give us guidance, but His complete guidance is usually confirmed as He uses *all* of these methods to speak His truth to us. We read something in the Word that speaks to us. We are reminded of general principles in God's Word, and we begin to see how they apply to our situation—perhaps through the message of a song or a sermon, the words of a friend, or a sudden recollection of passages we have read in God's Word previously. We see circumstances beginning to change around us. We feel the presence of the Holy Spirit in our lives, convicting us to turn from evil or His assurance we can embrace something that will be for our good.

The Holy Spirit does not want God's will for our lives be a mystery. He has come to reveal the truth to us. He has come in His all-knowing ability to impart to us what we need to know in order to live obedient and faithful lives. So trust Him to guide you . . . now and always!

7. "Whatever you do in word or deed, do all in the name of the Lord Jesus, giving thanks to God the Father through Him" (Colossians 3:17). What does it mean, in practical terms, to "do all in the name of the Lord Jesus"? Why are we commanded to give thanks to the Father even when we are serving Him?

....

....

....

....

....

....

....

8. "Be anxious for nothing, but in everything by prayer and suppli-cation, with thanksgiving, let your requests be made known to God; and the peace of God, which surpasses all understanding, will guard your hearts and minds through Christ Jesus" (Philip-pians 4:6–7). Why does Paul command us not to be anxious? Why does Paul add "with thanksgiving" to our prayers? Why is it important for us to be thankful to God?

....

....

....

....

....

....

....

....

MY FINAL WORD TO YOU

The Spirit-filled life. I opened this Bible study with those words, and I want to close with them. But let me add the word *wonderful* to this phrase: *the wonderful Spirit-filled life.* The life the Holy Spirit desires to impart to you can be described only as wonderful—wonderful in the many benefits you experience personally, wonderful in the many blessings that come to others around you, and wonderful in the sense that you are made more keenly aware of the glory and majesty of God the Father and Jesus Christ. The Spirit-filled life should be marked by awe—that you are indwelled by the Holy Spirit, who desires to use you in accomplishing His purposes on earth, and who longs to live with you forever in eternity.

Of course, the extent to which you live this wonderful Spirit-led life is up to you. I would urge you to choose today to rely on the Holy Spirit for every aspect of your life, in every decision or choice that you make, and during every hour of every day. Trust Him to work through you. Trust Him to mold you into the image of Christ Jesus. Trust Him to bless you as you have never been blessed before. As you ask Him to do His work in your life, you will receive His help and guidance—and in the process, you will manifest His character.

9. "Your ears shall hear a word behind you, saying, 'This is the way, walk in it,' whenever you turn to the right hand or whenever you turn to the left" (Isaiah 30:21). What major insights have you gained in this study of the Holy Spirit?

....
....
....
....
....
....
....
....

10. Where is God guiding you today? How has your relationship with His Spirit helped you to understand His leading?

....
....
....
....
....
....
....
....
....

TODAY AND TOMORROW

Today: The Holy Spirit wants to guide me into God's complete plan for my life.

Tomorrow: I will make myself fully available to follow and obey the Holy Spirit's direction.

Closing Prayer

Heavenly Father, we praise You for Your kindness and Your patience with us. Today, we ask that You remove any hardness that has developed in our heart about the work of the Holy Spirit. We pray that You would convict us and remind us to keep going in the direction that leads to life everlasting. Lord, we recognize that only the Holy Spirit knows what is fully good and right for us. Allow us to listen to the voice of the Spirit of truth so we can always be pointed in the direction of what Jesus would be, say, or do in any and every situation. Thank You, Lord. Amen.

Notes and
Prayer Requests

Use this space to write any key points, questions, or prayer requests from this week's study.

Leader's Guide

Thank you for choosing to lead your group through this Bible study from Dr. Charles F. Stanley on *Relying on the Holy Spirit*. The rewards of being a leader are different from those of participating, and it is our prayer that your own walk with Jesus will be deepened by this experience. During the twelve lessons in this study, you will be helping your group members explore key themes about how to depend on the Holy Spirit's guidance, while using Dr. Stanley's teachings and review questions to encourage group discussion. There are multiple components in this section that can help you structure your lessons and discussion time, so please be sure to read and consider each one.

Before You Begin

Before your first meeting, make sure your group members each have a copy of *Relying on the Holy Spirit* so they can follow along in the study guide and have their answers written out ahead of time. Alternately, you can hand out the study guides at your first meeting and give the group members some time to look over the material and ask any preliminary questions. During your first meeting, be sure to send a sheet around the room and have the members write down their name, phone number, and email address so you can keep in touch with them during the week.

To ensure everyone has a chance to participate in the discussion, the ideal size for a group is around eight to ten people. If there are more than ten people, break up the bigger group into smaller subgroups. Make sure the members are committed to participating each week, as this will help create stability and help you better prepare the structure of the meeting.

At the beginning of each meeting, you may wish to start the group time by asking the group members to provide their initial reactions to the material they have read during the week. The goal is to just get the group members' preliminary thoughts—so encourage them at this point to keep their answers brief. Ideally, you want everyone in the group to get a chance to share some of their thoughts, so try to keep the responses to a minute or less.

Give the group members a chance to answer, but tell them to feel free to pass if they wish. With the rest of the study, it's generally not a good idea to have everyone answer every question—a free-flowing discussion is more desirable. But with the opening icebreaker questions, you can go around the circle. Encourage shy people to share, but don't force them. Also, try to keep any one person from dominating the discussion so everyone will have the opportunity to participate.

Weekly Preparation

As the group leader, there are a few things you can do to prepare for each meeting:

- *Be thoroughly familiar with the material in the lesson.* Make sure you understand the content of each lesson so you know how to structure the group time and are prepared to lead the group discussion.

- *Decide, ahead of time, which questions you want to discuss.* Depending on how much time you have each week, you may not be able to reflect on every question. Select specific questions that you feel will evoke the best discussion.

- *Take prayer requests.* At the end of your discussion, take prayer requests from your group members and then pray for one another.

- *Pray for your group.* Pray for your group members through-out the week and ask that God would lead them as they study His Word.

- *Bring extra supplies to your meeting.* The members should bring their own pens for writing notes, but it's a good idea to have extras available for those who forget. You may also want to bring paper and additional Bibles.

TRUCTURING THE GROUP DISCUSSION TIME

You will need to determine with your group how long you want to meet each week so you can plan your time accordingly. Generally, most groups like to meet for either sixty minutes or ninety minutes, so you could use one of the following schedules:

SECTION	60 Minutes	90 Minutes
WELCOME (group members arrive and get settled)	5 minutes	10 minutes
ICEBREAKER (group members share their initial thoughts regarding the content in the lesson)	10 minutes	15 minutes
DISCUSSION (discuss the Bible study questions you selected ahead of time)	35 minutes	50 minutes
PRAYER/CLOSING (pray together as a group and dismiss)	10 minutes	15 minutes

As the group leader, it is up to you to keep track of the time and keep things moving according to your schedule. If your group is having a good discussion, don't feel the need to stop and move on to the next question. Remember, the purpose is to pull together ideas and share unique insights on the lesson. Encourage everyone to participate, but don't be concerned if certain group members are more quiet. They may just be internally reflecting on the questions and need time to process their ideas before they can share them.

GROUP DYNAMICS

Leading a group study can be a rewarding experience for you and your group members—but that doesn't mean there won't be challenges. Certain members may feel uncomfortable in discussing topics that they consider very personal and might be afraid of being called on. Some members might have disagreements on specific issues. To help prevent these scenarios, consider establishing the following ground rules:

- If someone has a question that may seem off topic, suggest that it is discussed at another time, or ask the group if they are okay with addressing that topic.

- If someone asks a question to which you do not know the answer, confess that you don't know and move on. If you feel comfortable, you can invite the other group members to give their opinions or share their comments based on personal experience.

- If you feel like a couple of people are talking much more than others, direct questions to people who may not have shared yet. You could even ask the more dominating members to help draw out the quiet ones.

- When there is a disagreement, encourage the members to process the matter in love. Invite members from opposing sides to evaluate their opinions and consider the ideas of the other members. Lead the group through Scripture that addresses the topic, and look for common ground.

When issues arise, encourage your group to follow these words from Scripture: "Love one another" (John 13:34), "If it is possible, as much as it depends on you, live peaceably with all men" (Romans 12:18), "Whatever things are true . . . noble . . . pure . . . lovely . . . if there is any virtue and if there is anything praiseworthy—meditate on these things" (Philippians 4:8), and "Be swift to hear, slow to speak, slow to wrath" (James 1:19). This will make your group time more rewarding and beneficial for everyone who attends.

Thank you again for your willingness to lead your group. May God reward your efforts and dedication, equip you to guide your group in the weeks ahead, and make your time together in *Relying on the Holy Spirit* fruitful for His kingdom.

Also Available in the
Charles F. Stanley Bible Study Series

The Charles F. Stanley Bible Study Series is a unique approach
to Bible study, incorporating biblical truth, personal insights,
emotional responses, and a call to action. Each study draws on
Dr. Stanley's many years of teaching the guiding principles found
in God's Word, showing how we can apply them in practical
ways to every situation we face. This edition of the series has
been completely revised and updated, and includes two
brand-new lessons from Dr. Stanley.

Advancing
Through Adversity
9780310106555

Experiencing
Forgiveness
9780310106579

Listening
to God
9780310106593

Relying on the
Holy Spirit
9780310106616

Available now at your favorite bookstore.
More volumes coming soon.

THOMAS NELSON
Since 1798